Robert Hammond, John Ashburnham

Letters Between Col. Robert Hammond

Governor of the Isle of Wight, and the committee of lords and commons at Derby-House, General Fairfax, Lieut. General Cromwell, Commissary General Ireton, &c. relating to King Charles I.

Robert Hammond, John Ashburnham

Letters Between Col. Robert Hammond
Governor of the Isle of Wight, and the committee of lords and commons at Derby-House, General Fairfax, Lieut. General Cromwell, Commissary General Ireton, &c. relating to King Charles I.

ISBN/EAN: 9783337409319

Printed in Europe, USA, Canada, Australia, Japan

Cover: Foto ©ninafisch / pixelio.de

More available books at **www.hansebooks.com**

LETTERS

BETWEEN

Col. ROBERT HAMMOND,
Governor of the *Isle of Wight*,

AND THE

Committee of LORDS and COMMONS
at *Derby-House*,
General FAIRFAX, Lieut. General CROMWELL,
Commissary General IRETON, &c.

RELATING TO

King CHARLES I.
While he was confined in *Carisbrooke-Castle*
in that Island.

NOW FIRST PUBLISHED.

To which is prefixed

A LETTER

FROM

JOHN ASHBURNHAM, Esq;

TO A FRIEND,

Concerning his Deportment towards the King, in his Attendance on his Majesty at *Hampton-Court*, and in the *Isle of Wight*.

PREFACE.

THE papers now offered to the public relate to so interesting an event in the *English* History not hitherto fully understood, that no apology seems necessary for taking this method of preserving authentic copies of them from the like unfortunate accident, that consumed the originals in the fire, which proved fatal to a great number of other valuable Manuscripts, in the chambers of the Hon. Mr. *Yorke*, in *Lincoln's-Inn*, on the 27th of *June*, 1752. The copies had been taken by the late Dr. *Joseph Letherland*,

land, Fellow of the Royal College of Physicians, *London*, and Physician in ordinary to her Majesty; his diligent search after all kinds of useful knowledge having led him to the study of history, especially that of his own country, of which he was as great a master, as of all other branches of learning and science. And his temper being as communicative, as it was amiable in all other respects, he had, after the loss of the originals, some thoughts of securing to the public these only copies known to be extant, by permitting them to be printed.

To render this collection as complete as possible, six other letters, which were part of the collection of Col. *Hammond*, are reprinted here from Mr. *Harris's Appendix* to his *Historical*

PREFACE.

Historical and critical account of the life of Oliver Cromwell.

THE circumstances of King *Charles* I's retreat in *November* 1647, from *Hampton-Court*, to the *Isle of Wight*, attended only by Sir *John Berkley*, Mr. *John Ashburnham*, and Col. *William Legge*, and his putting himself into the hands of Col. *Robert Hammond*, Governor of that island, may be seen, as represented by Sir *John Berkley* himself, in his *Memoirs*, printed in 1699; those of Mr. *Ashburnham* on the same subject, though perused, and referred to, by Lord *Clarendon**, not having yet seen the light. However, one may form some notion of his reasons for conducting the King to that island, from a pamphlet printed in the year 1648,

* History of the Rebellion, p. 511. edit. Oxford, 1732, fol.

but now grown extremely rare, and on that account reprinted here, intitled, "The true copy of a letter from Mr. *Ashburnham* to a friend, concerning his deportment towards the King in his late attendance upon his Majesty's person, at *Hampton-Court* and the *Isle of Wight*".

This Gentleman, who was honoured with a distinguished share of the confidence of his Royal Master, had been already employed by him in an application to the younger Sir *Henry Vane*, about three months before the King left *Oxford*, to go to the *Scots* Army, in *April* 1646, accompanied by Mr. *Ashburnham*. The design of this application appears from two curious papers, which the Editor transcribed from copies attested by his Majesty's own hand, and found among the

PREFACE.

the state-papers of Secretary *Nicholas*, left by the will of his grandson *William Nicholas*, Esq; to the late Sir *John Evelyn*, Bart. These, having not yet been printed, may not unsuitably be subjoined here.

"SIR,

"YOU cannot suppose the work
" is done, though God should
" suffer you to destroy the King.
" The miseries, which will inevitably
" follow, are so plain in view, that
" it is more than necessary some speedy
" expedient be found for their pre-
" vention. Is it not clear to you (to
" me it is) that *Spain* and *France*
" will instantly conclude a peace; and
" that *France* makes great prepara-
" tions to join with the *Scots*, when the
" breach between you and them shall
" happen, whilst *Spain* labours to be

protector

"protector of *Ireland*, and will un-
"doubtedly carry it? Confider well;
"whether the feafon is not proper
"for this defign, when the wealth
"of the nation is already fo exhaufted;
"and the fufferings of the people fo
"great, that they are no longer to be
"fupported. This is reafon: it is
"not to caft a bone amongft you.
"The only remedy is, and it is a fafe
"and honourable one for you, that
"you fet yourfelf, the gentleman, that
"was quartered with you, and all his
"and your friends, to prevail, that
"the King may come to *London* up-
"on the terms he hath offered *;

* In the end of *January* 1645-6, his Majefty fent a letter to the Parliament, urging, what he had propounded in the end of the preceding month, his coming to *London* for a perfonal treaty, and offering the Militia to be fettled in their hands for feven years; that they fhould nominate the officers of ftate, judges, &c. that religion fhould be fet-

where

PREFACE.

"where if Presbytery should be so
"strongly insisted upon, as that there
"can be no peace without it, you
"shall certainly have all the power
"my master can make, to join with
"you in rooting out of this kingdom
"that tyrannical government; with
"this condition, that my master may
"not have his conscience disturbed
"(yours being free) when that easy
"work is finished. Lose not this fair
"opportunity; the like was never of-
"fered, nor ever will be; for it brings
"all things of benefit and advantage
"imaginable, both to the general and
"your particular, to him, that was
"quartered with you, and to his and
"your friends, and shall be honestly
tled as in the days of Queen *Elizabeth*, having
regard to tender conscience: and that with regard to *Ireland*, and the other propositions, he
would grant what had been offered at the treaty
of *Uxbridge*.

"made

PREFACE.

" made good. Truſt to me for the
" performance of it. Weigh it ſad-
" ly, and again rely upon me. Be
" confident, that neither he that
" carries, nor he that delivers it to
" you, knows any thing of it.

*This is a trew coppie of what was
ſent to Sir* Henry Vane, *the younger,
by my command.*   C. R.
March 2. 1645.

" SIR,
" I SHALL only add this word
" to what was ſaid in my laſt, that
" you haſten my buſineſs all that poſ-
" ſibly you can, the occaſion lately
" given being fairer than ever, and
" done on purpoſe. Be very con-
" fident, that all things ſhall be per-
" formed according to my promiſe.
" By all that is good, I conjure you
" to

PREFACE. xi

"to difpatch that courtefy for me
"with all fpeed, or it will be too late.
"I fhall perifh before I receive the
"fruits of it. I may not tell you
"my neceffities; but if it were ne-
"ceffary fo to do, I am fure you
"would lay all other confiderations a-
"fide, and fulfill my defires. This
"is all: truft me, I will repay your
"favour to the full. I have done. If
"I have not an anfwer within four
"days after the receipt of this, I fhall
"be neceffitated to find fome other ex-
"pedient. God direct you. I have
"difcharged my duty."

This is a true coppie of what was fent by Jack Afhburnham, *and my command, to* Sir Harry Vane, *the younger.*   C. R.

CONTENTS

CONTENTS.

A LETTER from Mr. *Ashburnham* to a Friend concerning his Deportment towards the King in his late attendance upon his Majesty's Person at *Hampton-Court* and the *Isle of Wight*   Page 1

I. The Committee of the Admiralty to Col. *Hammond*   17

II. Commissary-General *Ireton* to Col. *Hammond*   19

III. Lieut. Gen. *Cromwell* to Col. *Hammond*   23

IV. The Committee at *Derby-House* to Col. *Hammond*   26

V. The same Committee to Col. *Hammond*   28

VI. The same Committee to Col. *Hammond*   30

VII. General *Fairfax* to Col. *Hammond*   31

VIII. The Committee at *Derby-House* to Col. *Hammond*   33

IX. Proceedings of the Committee, for taking the Accompts of the Ordnance of the Kingdom   34

CONTENTS.

X. The Committee of the Admiralty to Col. *Hammond*   35

XI. The Committee at *Derby-Houfe* to Col. *Hammond*   36

XII. The fame Committee to Col. *Hammond*   37

XIII. *Art. Hafelrige*, and others, to Col. *Hammond*   39

XIV. Lieut. General *Cromwell*, to Col. *Hammond*   40

XV. Mr. *Froft*, Secretary of the Committee, at *Derby-Houfe*, to Col. *Hammond*   42

XVI. An Anonymous Friend to Col. *Hammond*   44

XVII. Another   45

XVIII. Another   46

XIX. Another   48

XX. Col. *Hammond* to the Committee of Lords and Commons   51

XXI. Mr. *Froft* to Col. *Hammond*   61

XXII. The Committee at *Derby-Houfe*, to Col. *Hammond*   62

XXIII. Inftructions from Col. *Hammond* to Major *Rolph*, &c.   64

XXIV. The Committee at *Derby-Houfe*, to Col. *Hammond*   66

CONTENTS.

XXV. The same Committee to Col. *Hammond*   68

XXVI. Col. *Hammond* to the Committee of Lords and Commons   69

XXVII. Col. *Hammond* to the General *Thomas* Lord *Fairfax*   72

XXVIII. Mr. *Frost* to Col. *Hammond*   74

XXIX. Mr. *Frost* to Col. *Hammond*   76

XXX. The Committee at *Derby-House*, to Col. *Hammond*   78

XXXI. Commissary-General *Ireton* to Col. *Hammond*   79

XXXII. The Committee at *Derby-House* to Col. *Hammond*   81

XXXIII. The same Committee to Col. *Hammond*   83

XXXIV. The same Committee to Col. *Hammond*   85

XXXV. Commissary-General *Ireton*, Major *Harrison*, Col. *Desbrowe*, and Col. *Grosvenor*, to Col. *Hammond*   87

XXXVI. The Committee at *Derby-House* to Col. *Hammond*   90

XXXVII. Commissary-General *Ireton* to Col. *Hammond*   95

XXXVIII. *Oliver Cromwell* to Col. *Hammond*   101

A

LETTER

FROM

Mr. ASHBURNHAM,

TO

A FRIEND,

Concerning his Deportment towards the KING in his late Attendance upon his Majesty's Person at *Hampton-Court* and the *Isle of Wight*.

First printed in the YEAR 1648.

A LETTER

FROM

Mr. ASHBURNHAM, *to a* FRIEND, *&c.*

SIR,

I HAVE withheld this return too long; of which I am by so much the more ashamed, by how much I found yours so full of kindness. I will pretend to no excuse; but if your good nature will suggest, that the deep sense of my afflictions doth so oppress my spirits, as it renders me altogether indisposed to the least intercourse, you will be charitable, and take me right.

Would you believe, that, to my sorrows for the sufferings of our dear master the King, and the danger of the public, the generality of men in this kingdom (and probably in many other parts too) should charge me with the scandal of having betrayed his

Majesty into the *Isle of Wight*, and that by compact with the Parliament and Army before his departure from *Hampton-Court?* And, to obtain belief the better, have digested that their calumny into this form; that I did conspire with them to affright his Majesty away from thence, that they might have the better opportunity, being at a greater distance from *London*, to destroy him; which to effect, the nearness of that place made it very difficult, if not impossible; and that my reward for this service hath been a great sum of money? Thus from several hands.

Which reproach, though I never deserved, and take myself to be very much above any thing of that kind: yet since there is no person, ambitious to acquire or preserve an honest reputation, but is awake, and always carries about him a tenderness to the least prejudice or diminution thereof; I cannot but be touched with some sense of that unhappy report, and give you, in whose good esteem I am much concerned, the true state of my part in that action,
so

so far as may enable you to satisfy, if you meet with him, the most malicious person against me.

THAT I was commanded by their Majesties and the Prince's Highness to return into *England*, with instructions to endeavour, by the best means imaginable, such a compliance between his Majesty and the Army, as might have influence, and beget a right understanding between his Majesty and the Parliament, is a truth well known. That my infirmities are so great, and so public, as that it had been better for their service to have given that employment to some other of more eminent endowments, I do acknowledge with great humility. But that I did fulfill that trust with all industry and fidelity to their Majesties, I appeal to God and them, and do not doubt but I have my portion of favour, and stand still numbered in the catalogue of those subjects, whom they are yet pleased to stile faithful.

WHAT passed between me and any member either of the Parliament or Army, as it will not at all advantage his Majesty's affairs to relate, so will it not any way conduce to my vindication. This word I shall only let fall, that a wiser man than I, or whoever is my greatest censurer, would and ought to have given credit to them, when power and interest, accompanied with large expressions of good will, were the arguments and motives to gain belief of their real intentions. Nay truly, though his Majesty had known they intended nothing less than the performance of those duties to their Sovereign and country, I cannot find (I know not what a quicker-sighted man might have done) how in prudence his Majesty could have pursued any other interest, or made any other application, than what he did, considering the power under which he was: Which shall serve by way of glance at my part of negotiation in general, because even therein likewise I am not without some prejudice in many mens conceptions.

Some few weeks before his Majesty's remove from *Hampton-Court*, there was scarce a day a day, in which several alarms were not brought to his Majesty, by and from very considerable persons (both well affected to him, and likely to know much of what was then in agitation) of the resolution, which a violent party in the Army had to take away his life: And that such a design there was, there were strong inducements to perswade; and I hope charity will be afforded to those many, who were and still are of that belief, since I confess myself to be of that number. Which practice seemed to his Majesty the more probable, for that many other particulars, which were said in those informations to precede that action, fell out accordingly. Whereupon his Majesty thought it not wisdom longer to despise the possible means left him for the prevention of that danger; and therefore resolved to retire himself from thence, but with this positive intention, not to desert this kingdom, either by crossing the seas, or going into *Scotland*. The reasons his Majesty gave, you will pardon me if I deliver not; and suspend your censure, in case your judgement invite you to oppose that result, till you hear the weight of them.

them; and I will ingage the little credit the world hath left me, you shall be satisfied.

And what man is he, who hath the least grain of understanding, bears about him any affections either to his sacred person, or to the common good, hath any regard to his own duty or reputation, would have taken upon him to dissuade his Majesty from what he had then resolved on ; and thereby exposed himself both to the danger and guilt of that mischief, which so many had forewarned him of, and was so likely to happen? Sure I am, if I had been that man, I should have thought myself justly to have merited the character of unfaithfulness, which is now so injuriously cast upon me.

It rested then, that his Majesty was to make choice of a place, where he might avoid the present danger; where he might give least offence to the interest of the Parliament and Army; where he might have frequent intercourse with both, for settling a peace, of which he then despaired not; and, lastly, where he might most securely

(and

(and the meafure of fafety was, where there were no foldiers) expect the abatement of the ruinous power of the levellers and their faction to be the fruits of the general rendezvous, which was immediately to follow.

UPON thefe grounds, his Majefty thought the *Ifle of Wight* moft proper for his refidence, efpecially if he could obtain honourable conditions from the governor of that place; to whom (when his Majefty was come within twenty miles) he commanded Sir *John Berkley* and myfelf to repair, and make trial of what reception we could procure for him; who, after fome confideration of what we propofed, proffered this engagement, That, *fince it appeared his Majefty came from* Hampton-Court *to fave his life, if he pleafed to put himfelf into his hands, whatever he could expect from a perfon of honour or honefty, his Majefty fhould have it made good by him:* Which truely to us feemed fufficient; and I do for my own part acknowledge, my confidence was, that, by that engagement, he would not have laid any reftraint upon his Majefty, nor have given

given accefs to any foldiers into that ifland. But how honourably and how faithfully he hath performed his promifed duty to the King, you are as good a witnefs as myfelf; and therefore, as I take little pleafure in the memory of it, fo there will be little fatisfaction to you in repeating it. It fhall fuffice, that I have now been taught, that honour and honefty have clear contrary definitions in feveral men's underftandings.

For the election his Majefty made of the *Ifle of Wight,* upon the grounds before mentioned, as therewith I did then concur, fo, with refpect to their judgements, who are otherwife perfwaded, I do ftill believe it was, as his affairs then ftood, the beft of any place, which he could make choice of. And I will not be afraid to avow my opinion, becaufe fuccefs hath made it feem lefs reafonable; which being taken out of the fcale, and all circumftances worthy debate, before his departure from *Hampton-Court,* confidered; perhaps wifer men than thofe, who in that prefume to condemn his Majefty's

Majesty's judgement, may yet approve of that choice. However, his Majesty was resolved to go from *Hampton-Court*; and, I know not what other men's customs are, I cannot but be well satisfied with my own, which hath been ever ready to submit, when his Majesty hath been willing to command. And I should account it a great misfortune to me, that his commands should be such, to which I should think fit rather with humility to oppose my reasons, than with chearfulness to obey his pleasure. But that strait hath never yet happened, nor, I am confident, ever will; so careful is his Majesty to impose nothing upon any man, but what he believes just and lawful.

That any member of the Parliament or Army had any knowledge by me of his Majesty's removal from *Hampton-Court*, or that any compact between me and any of them was ever made, to the disservice of his Majesty in any particular whatsoever, I provoke them and all the world to produce the least colour of proof; and desire, that no man would spare me more than I
should

should do such, whom I found guilty of so base a crime; and shall not stick to invite them to it, who have been so liberal in blasting my reputation, when I may live with that freedom they do, which either their greater wisdom, or their less loyalty than mine, hath purchased. In the mean time, it is some comfort to me to find these censurers to be men but of such dispositions, as will hazard no more than only their good wishes for his Majesty; and for such I take them, and for such leave them.

IF I should tell these severe judges of other men's actions, that his Majesty's present personal condition is the same in the *Isle of Wight* with what it was, when he left *Hampton-Court*, they would perhaps wonder at me, but upon examination find it truth: for before his Majesty's coming from thence, at least six days, he was forbidden riding abroad, and confined within the limits of that place.

AND if any man can assure me, that if his Majesty had continued at *Hampton-Court,*

Court, the Parliament would not have pre‑ sented these four bills to him *, or that, they being presented, his Majesty's refusing to make them laws, should not have drawn on his late restraint, or the later votes of Parliament concerning farther application to his Majesty †. I shall then (for indeed I take that to be the cause of his relapse) with great lowliness of spirit acknowledge my‑ self to have been an unhappy (though not an unfaithful) instrument in his Majesty's remove from *Hampton-Court.* But till then, my sufferings in these scandals may be continued, but my opinion not changed, nor the quietness of my mind disturbed, for having in that action discharged my duty to his Majesty.

As for the money I should have received for betraying his Majesty, if none of my Calumniators have more to subsist on, than I have had either from Parliament or Army,

* Presented to the King in the latter end of *Decem‑ ber* 1647.

† The votes for no more addresses to his Majesty, pas‑ sed the House of Commons on the 3d of *January* 1647-8.

they

they would be in worse condition, than, notwithstanding all their malice to me, I wish them. In earnest, it would better have become those, who first designed me this infamy, to have made choice of some, who had a mark upon them for doing some action, which may at least be of kin to the accusation, though but between fellow-subjects: but you will pardon my vanity, if I say I abhor such unworthiness, and defy mankind to bring the least blemish of that nature in judgement against me.

I have done, when I have told you, that I have heard divines say, that God doth most punish us in those things we most prize, and think ourselves most concerned. I shall therefore hope to make a religious use of these aspersions cast upon my integrity; for I fear I did glory too much in my honour of faithfulness and and loyalty to his Majesty, and did not thankfully consider, as I ought to have done, that it was the blessing of God, which enabled

enabled me to go thorough with the performance of my duty in his service.

If men would but as well think upon the solicitude and care of their minds, who are honoured with near relations to the service of great Princes, as they look upon the advantages, which thereby fortune may cast upon them, they would find more cause to pity them for their labour and hazards, which is ordinarily beyond their capacities to fathom, who are at very remote distance, than to envy them for their honour or profit. But since of all evils seated in the heart of man, malice hath the greatest dominion, it were vain for virtue itself to hope for freedom from those effects, which naturally arise from it; and much more for me, who, though in this particular I have as much innocence to protect me, as can be consistent with mortality, yet in other things, which may be imputed to weakness, and unskilfulness in matters of great concernment, I do with all ingenuity confess, no man carries a greater weight of guilt than he, whose care it is, to preserve unspotted the reputation of an honest man, thereby to retain still the favour and affection, wherewith you have constantly honoured,

S I R,

Your most faithful, and

Most humble servant,

JOHN ASHBURNHAM.

LETTERS

BETWEEN

Col. *Robert Hammond*, Governor of the *Isle of Wight*, and the Committee of Lords and Commons at *Derby-House*, General *Fairfax*, Lieut. General *Cromwell*, Commissary General *Ireton*, &c.

LETTER I.

The Committee of the Admiralty to Col. Robert Hammond (a).

Col. *Hammond*,

YOUR letter of the 6th of *November* came to our hands yesterday; by which we understand your great care and vigilance in the service of the state, in staying

(a) He was born the year 1621, and second son of *Robert Hammond*, of *Chertsey*, in *Surrey*, Esq; elder brother of that eminent divine Dr. *Henry Hammond*, and son of Dr. *John Hammond*, physician to Prince *Henry*. Col. *Hammond* was entered a commoner of *Magdalen-Hall*, in the university of *Oxford*, in the year 1636, and having continued there three years,

B   left

ſtaying of capt. *Falkner* and his veſſel, with the *French* veſſel, which he brought into the *Cowes,* as his prize. We deſire you to continue your reſtraint on the ſaid *Falkner's* veſſel and company, and likewiſe the *French,* until you receive farther order

left the univerſity without the honour of a degree: Upon the breaking out of the war in 1642 he engaged in arms on the ſide of the Parliament, by the perſauſion of his uncle *Thomas Hammond,* then captain of horſe, and afterwards lieutenant general of the ordnance, by whoſe intereſt his nephew was made a captain, then major under col. *Edward Maſſey,* during the ſiege of *Gloucester,* in the courſe of which he killed major *Gray* for giving him the lie; on which he was ordered by the Houſe of Commons to be tried by the council of war in the lord general's army; (*Whitelock's Memorials,* p. 106. edit. 1732,) by whom he appears to have been acquitted. He was at laſt raiſed to the rank of colonel of a regiment of foot, in which he continued till the end of the war; and on the 6th of *September* 1647, was appointed governor of the *Iſle of Wight,* which poſt he executed till towards the 20th of *November* 1648, when he was ordered by the general *Thomas* lord *Fairfax* to reſign the cuſtody of the King to lieut. col. *Iſaac Ewre,* and to repair to the head quarters at *Windſor.* In the year 1654 he was ſent to *Ireland,* where he arrived in *September* of that year, as appears from *Thurloe's State-papers,* vol. II. p. 602; but he died on the 24th of the month following at *Dublin,* where he was one of the Parliament's commiſſioners. *Whitelocke,* p. 607.

from

from this committee; and that you will give special charge to your under-officers, to take care, that none of the goods belonging to the said *French* prize be embezelled, or taken away. So we kindly salute you, and rest

From the committee of lords and commissioners for the Admiralty and Cinque-ports sitting at *Westminster*, this 11th of *Nov.* 1647.

To our very loving friend col. *Robt. Hammond*, governor of the *Isle of Wight*, and Vice Admiral of *Hampshire*, &c.

Your very loving

friends;

Warwicke.
E. Manchester.
Denis Bond.
John Lisle.
Tho. Rainberowe.
Alex. Bence.

LETTER II.

Commissary General *Ireton*, to Col. *Robert Hammond.*

Dear *Hammond,*

THAT thou hast not had more frequent letters from us, since the trouble that has fallen upon thee, thou wouldst think it excusable, if thou knewest the burden and distractions, which ever since we have otherwise undergone; though now,

through

through the goodness of God, we are at more ease and quiet. And though thou hast had no scribbling from my hand, yet it hath not been wanting in that care, that hath been taken for thee; or that little, that hath been written to thee. For present matter of advice, first in the business concerning Mr. *Ashburnham*, &c. I fully concur with the general's letter, that it is fit they be sent up, as 'tis ordered. Next concerning admission of chaplains and other persons to the King, &c. according to former civilities, I cannot think them safe to be allowed in that place, or in the condition you are in. And I think, as we never had obligation to it (but did it freely) so now much less. For the pretence of the king's keeping himself within the protection of the army by coming into your hands; both reason, and all the circumstances I have heard, make me believe, and the King's own declaration, left behind upon his table, doth plainly discover, that he in his going away had other intentions; and his surrendring himself to you was besides his first purpose. And I cannot

cannot believe, but it was a second counsel, and that, tho' appearingly a choice, yet really upon some emergent necessity, for the avoiding of a worse, when he someway found himself stopt, and unable to get clear away, according to his first intention. Now for your better securing the King, and making sure the island, to prevent any danger to the kingdom, which a confluence or appearance of ill-affected persons there might occasion, I advise you by no means to trust so wholly to the affections of islanders, but take in soldiers, whom you may have more surely at command; for which purpose we have ordered some to you, and shall send more. In the mean time I pray you neglect not to send for those ordered from *Southampton*; and we shall take care, those you take into the island, upon this occasion, shall be paid, while they stay there, whatever others are.

WE are earnest with *Harrison* [b] to come over to thee for assistance in the way of advice; and I hope he will come.

[b] *Tho. Harrison*, son of a butcher or grazier of *Newcastle under Line* in *Staffordshire*, and educated

DEAR *Robin*, I must tell thee, God hath wonderfully appeared to justify and bear witness to that little measure of integrity and truth, which he hath given to his servants. And I am confident, he will appear with us still; untill he bring us off the stage without reproach or scandal to his name. To his direction and good pleasure I commit thee in the great charge and burthen he hath brought upon thee, even in that place, where thou hadst, I believe, promised thyself nothing but ease and quiet: and in him I remain

Thine most affectionately,

Windsor, Nov. 21. 1647.   H. Ireton.

 The Lieut. General (*c*) is at *London* or *Putney*, and on scout I know not where. I have opened thy letters to them, and read and shall deliver them, when they come.

as an attorney at Cliffords-Inn, who, having taken arms against the king, raised himself to the rank of colonel, and at last of major-general. He was one of his majesty's judges at his tryal, for which he was executed at Tyburn, 13 *October* 1660.

 (*c*) *Oliver Cromwell.*

LETTER

LETTER III.

Lieut. General *Cromwell* to Col. *Hammond.*

Deareſt *Robin*,

NOW (bleſſed be God) I can write, and thou receive, freely. I never in my life ſaw more deep ſenſe, and leſs will to ſhew it unchriſtianly, than in that, which thou didſt write to us, when we were at *Windſor*, and thou in the midſt of thy temptation, which indeed (by what we underſtood of it) was a great one, and occaſioned the greater by the letter the general ſent thee, of which thou waſt not miſtaken, when thou didſt challenge me to be the penner.

How good has God been to diſpoſe all to mercy! and although it was trouble for the preſent, yet glory is come out of it, for which we praiſe the Lord with thee and for thee: and truely thy carriage has been ſuch, as occaſions much honour to the name of God and to religion. Go on in the ſtrength of the Lord, and the Lord be ſtill with thee. But, dear *Robin*, this buſineſs hath been (I truſt) a mighty providence to this poor kingdom and to us all. The House of Commons is very sensible of the King's dealings, and of our brethrens, in this late transaction. You should do well, if you have any thing, that may discover juggling, to search it out, and let us know it. It may be of admirable use at this time, because we shall (I hope) instantly go upon business in relation to them, tending to prevent danger. The House of Commons has this day voted as follows;—1st. They will make no more addresses to the King. 2*dly*. None shall apply to him without leave of the two houses, upon pain of being guilty of high treason. 3*dly*. They will receive nothing from the King, nor shall any other bring any thing to them from him, nor receive any thing from the King. *Lastly*, The members of both houses, who were of the committee of both kingdoms, are established in all that power in themselves, for *England* and *Ireland*, which they had to act with both kingdoms; and Sir *John Evelyn*, of *Wilts* (*d*), is added in

---

(*d*) He was afterwards appointed one of the council of

the

the room of Mr. *Recorder* (*e*); and *Nath. Fiennes* in the room of Sir *Philip Stapleton* (*f*); and my lord of *Kent* (*g*), in the

state, with general *Monk* at the head of it, on the 23d of *February* 1659-60, Bp. *Kennet's Register and Chronicle*, p. 66.

(*e*) *John Glynne*, Esq; educated at *Hart Hall*, in *Oxford*. He had been one of the managers of the House of Commons at the tryal of the earl of *Strafford*; and was himself one of the eleven members impeached of high treason by the Army, on the 16th of *June* 1647; and in *January* following deprived of his place of recorder of *London*: but in *October* 1648 made a serjeant at law. In *June* 1655 he was appointed by the Protector *Oliver Cromwell* lord chief justice of the upper bench, and afterwards one of the lords of the other house. He was chosen knight of the shire for the county of *Caernarvon* in the Parliament, which began at *Westminster*, 25th of *April* 1660, and after the restoration made on the 8th of *November* 1660 the king's oldest serjeant at law, and on the 16th of that month had the honour of knighthood. He died at his house in *Portugal Row*, *Lincoln's Inn Fields*, *November* 15, 1666.

(*f*) He had distinguished himself by his bravery at the battle of *Newbury*; but was afterwards one of the eleven members impeached by the Army in *June* 1647; upon which he retired to *Calais*, where he died soon after. *Whitelocke*, p. 256, 257. edit. 1732.

(*g*) *Henry* earl of *Kent*, who was appointed by the Parliament one of the commissioners of the Great Seal on the 15th of *March* 1647, and died in *April* 1649.

room of the earl of *Essex*. I think it good you take notice of this, the sooner the better. Let us know, how it is with you in point of strength, and what you need from us. Some of us think the King well with you, and that it concerns us to keep that island in great security, because of the *French*, &c. and, if so, where can the King be better? If you have more force, you will be sure of full provision for them. The lord bless thee: pray for

My lord *Wharton*'s, *Thy dear friend and servant*,
near ten at night,
Jan. 3. 1647. O. Cromwell.

For Col. *Robt. Hammond*, Governor of the *Isle of Wight*, these, for the service of the kingdom, haste, post haste.

Oliver Cromwell.

LETTER IV.
The Committee at *Derby House*, to Col. Hammond.

SIR,

THERE is now a Committee settled at *Derby House*, who are under an oath of secrecy; to whom therefore you may safely communicate any intelligence.

For

For the better concealing of what you shall write, we shall send you a cypher by the next messenger, this being to give you notice, that we have certain intelligence, that there are plottings and contrivances in hand to convey away the King; and that Sir *John Berkley* and Mr. *Ashburnham* are, or lately were, at *Netley Castle*, whither the King's party makes continual resort unto them about some such purpose. We are also informed, that the King hath constant intelligence given him of all things, which he receives by the hands of a woman, who bringeth it to him, when she bringeth his clean linen; of which we thought fit to give you this information, not doubting, but you will take the best care, that may be, to improve this notice to the advantage of the public.

> *Signed in the name, and by the warrant, of the Committee of Derby House, by your very loving friend,*

Derby House, 20 *January* 1647.

For Col. R. *Hammond*, Governor of the *Isle of Wight*.

E. Manchester.

Die

Die Martis 25 *Januarii*, 1647.

Resolved,

THAT it be referred to the Committee of *Derby House*, to consider of the desires of the governor of the *Isle of Wight*, in relation to the security of the person of the King; and that what the effecting those desires shall come to, they the said Committee of *Derby House* do charge upon the Committee of the Army, to give order for the issuing of the same, not exceeding the sum of one thousand pounds.

H. Elsynge,

Cler. Parl. Dom. Comm.

LETTER V.

The Committee at *Derby House* to Col. *Hammond.*

SIR,

WE have received your letter from *Carisbrook* of the 23d inst. and as to the want of fortification of the castle, the House

Houfe hath taken order for one thoufand pounds to be charged upon the Committee for the Army, which we have accordingly done, and defired them to fend it you forthwith; and we withall fend you the copy of the order of the Houfe for your direction for the difburfement and difpofing thereof. And whereas you fay, you do believe the King hath intelligence; but know not where to lay it; in our laft we gave you particular notice, that it was by the woman, that brings him his clean linen, which we again recommend to your care; and alfo, that you ufe your utmoft diligence for the fecurity of the King's perfon. We fhall take a view of the powers you have already for that purpofe; and, if we find any defect, we fhall move the houfe for a fupply.

Signed in the name, and by the warrant, of the Committee at Derby Houfe, by your affectionate friend,

Derby Houfe, 25
January 1647.

H. Kent.

LETTER

LETTER VI.

The Committee at Derby House, to Col. Hammond.

SIR,

WE have received your letter of the 28th inst. wherein you desire to have the approbation of this committee concerning the four gentlemen (*b*), by you appointed to watch in their courses at the King's chamber door. We think it fit, that in this business you should make your application to the houses (*i*), from whom, we doubt not, you will receive orders in that particular. For the money appointed for the fortification of the castle, it was to be furnished by the Committee of the Army by the appointment of this Committee, which

---

(*b*) Mr. *Tho. Herbert*, Mr. *Mildmay*, Capt. *Titus*, and Mr. *Preston*. *Rushworth*, part ii. vol. II. p. 992.

(*i*) Col. *Hammond*, having written accordingly to that purpose, was on the 18th of *February* 1647-8, impowered to place and displace such persons, as were to attend the King, as he should see occasion. *Rush-worth*, p. 1184.

which accordingly they presently did, and desired them to send thither with all speed: and of this information hath been given to the gentleman you mention, who solicits your business; which is all, that can be done at this committee for it.

>*Signed in the name, and by the warrant, of the Committee at Derby House, by your affectionate friend,*
>
>W. Say and Seal.

Derby House, 31 *January* 1647.
For Col. *Robt.* Hammond, governor of the *Isle of Wight*, these are.

LETTER VII.

General *Fairfax* to Col. *Hammona.*

SIR,

YOU see, by these einclosed votes, how great a burthen the Parliament hath laid upon me. I do hereby send to you, that you would instantly send me a list of such, as are at present about the King, who are persons fit to be confided in. If you have any in the island worthy of that trust,

* Of *Febr.* 2, 1647. *Whitelocke*, p. 290.

I would

I would desire you to send their names also in the same list: And if you cannot fill up the number of thirty with you, which I should be glad you could, then I desire you to send me the quality of those, that will be wanting, that so they may be supplyed from hence. It will be necessary, that you hasten this business, seeing the Parliament expects a speedy and effectual observance of their command herein. I purpose, so soon as I have received your list, to make the number up, and lay it before the Parliament, to receive their approbation and allowance for my indemnity. You see by the votes, That the number of thirty, of all sorts, gentlemen, their servants, cooks, butlers, &c. may not be exceeded; and therefore it will be fit, that a respect be had to all occasions and necessities of the houshold. Wishing you all success in your great trust and charge, I rest

Queenstreet, 5°   *Your assured friend*,
February 1647.

To Col. Robert Hammond, *Governor of the* Isle *of* Wight.   T. Fairfax.

LETTER

LETTER VIII.

The Committee at *Derby House*, to Col. Hammond. In Cypher.

SIR,

HAVING received some intelligence from a very good hand, which we have formerly found true, we thought it necessary to give you notice of it, and recommend the business to your especial care, that the King's escape is designed. The manner thus; by one *Napier* and a servant of *David Murray*, whom we take to be the King's tailor. The King is to be drawn up out of his bed chamber into the room over it, the ceiling whereof is to be broke for that purpose; and then conveyed from one room to another, till he be past all the rooms, where any guard are at any doors or windows.

Signed in the name, and by the warrant, of the committee at Derby House, by your very loving friend,

H. Kent,

Derby House, 7th *February* 1647.

To Col. Robert Hammond, *Governor of the* Isle of Wight.

LETTER IX.

At the Committee for taking the Accompts of the Ordnance of the Kingdom, &c.

Feb. 7°. 1647.

WHEREAS divers pieces of brass ordnance, heretofore belonging to Sir *William Waller's* train, are now remaining in the town of *Pool*, whereof two pieces of 6 pound bullet, two sakers, and eight three pounds, are thought fit to be removed into the *Isle of Wight*, for the defence thereof: It is therefore ordered, that the 12 pieces before mentioned be accordingly delivered unto such persons, as Col. *Hammond*, governor of the said island, shall appoint to remove and transport the same: For the doing whereof this shall be your sufficient warrant.

To the Mayor of the Town and County of Pool, *and to the Governor there.*

Wa. Erle,
Rob. Scawen,
Tho. Hodges,
Wm. Leman,
John Venne.

LETTER X.

The Committee of the Admiralty to Col. *Robert Hammond.*

SIR,

ON *Tuesday* last we received your letter of the 19th of *February*; and are putting it into a speedy way to bring the prisoners at *Winchester* to trial. The commission had been ere this time perfected, but that we have been expecting a report from the Admiralty, which came in but this day. We have also sent to the court of Admiralty, to know what proceedings have been had about the *Spanish* hull, at the *West Cowes*, and have taken order, in case she has not been already sentenced, to bring her to judgment in that court, that she may be thereupon disposed of according to justice. And so, with our affectionate salutations remembered, we rest,

Your affectionate friends,

By the Committee of Lords and Commons for the Admiralty and Cinque Ports, sitting at Westminster, *the* 2d *day of* March, 1647.

Warwick,
Salisbury,
Wa. Erle,
Denis Bond,
Giles Grene.

To our worthy friend Col. Rob. Hammond, *Vice-Admiral of the County of* Hants, *and Governor of the* Isle of Wight, *at* Carisbrooke-Castle.

LETTER XI.

The Committee at *Derby House* to Col. Hammond. In CYPHER.

SIR,

WE have received information, that there are now some designs in agitation concerning the King's escape, who is to be carried into *France*; and that there are two of those, that now attend the King, upon whom they rely for effecting this escape. Who they are we cannot discover, nor yet what grounds they have to expect their service in it: yet we thought fit to give you this advertisement, that you might the more carefully watch against it.

Signed in the name, and by the warrant, of the Committee sitting at Derby House, by your very loving friend,

Derby House, 13°.
Martii 1647.

A. Northumberland.

LETTER

LETTER XII.

The Committee at *Derby House*, to Col. Hammond.

SIR,

WE have received your letter of the 12th inst. with the note inclosed. And as to the five hundred men you desire to draw over, upon occasion, out of the next forces, the General hath given order therein to Col. *Ewer*; and for matter of money, there is a warrant signed for six hundred pounds by the Committee of the Army to be paid unto you. We have likewise spoken with some of the Committee of the Revenue, and they have signed a warrant for one thousand pounds, to be paid upon the order of thirty pounds a day; out of which thirty pounds a day, and by the discourse we have had, it is conceived there will be means for the entertainment of two hundred men. For it is conceived ten pounds a day will furnish the charge of the King's table: and the pay for 200 men with their officers in two companies, comes to about nine pounds more. And thirty shillings a day being allowed for your own table, there will remain nine pound ten shillings *per diem*, for extraordinary occasions, which is conceived may be sufficient for that purpose. But if there be a mistake in the compute, we desire you to give information of it to those, to whom it most properly belongs. As to the allowance you desire to be given to the four gentlemen your letter speaks of, although it be not the business of this Committee; yet, if you shall send the names of those gentlemen, and what it is you desire for them, we shall represent it to those, whom it concerns. For the victualling of that Castle and *Sandham Fort*, we shall make a report thereof to the houses.

Signed in the name, and by the warrant, of the Committee at Derby House, by your affectionate friend.

Derby House, 16°
Martii 1647-8.

P. Wharton.

For Col. *Rob. Hammond*, Governor of the *Isle of Wight*.

LETTER XIII.

To Col. *Hammond.*

SIR,

WE have received your letter, and, according to your defire, have herein fent you orders for three months affefment in the ifland for payment of the foldiery there. In your letter you mention, that you have made your company 200 men, which we leave to your difcretion: only we cannot affign payment for more than is within the compafs of the eftablifhment; but perhaps that may be fupplied out of the revenue. Concerning the guns, we have fent to Lieut. Col. *Reade,* Governor of *Pool,* who affirms to us, that they are old, and produces a certificate from his lieutenant and the gunner there. However we have appointed him fpeedily to repair to *Pool,* and to caufe the fame to be delivered (if they are not delivered already) according to the former order, for which purpofe we defire you to send for them; and we are assured you shall speedily receive them. We remain

Your very loving friends,

For Col. *R. Hammond.*

For the special service of Parliament.

Art. Hasilrige.
Rob. Scawen.
Thomas Pury.
Fran. Allein.
Edw. Prideaux.

LETTER XIV.

Lieut. General *Cromwell* to Col. *Hammond.*
In Cypher.

Dear Robin,

YOUR business is done in the house: your ten pounds by the week is made twenty pounds : 1000*l.* given you, and order to Mr. *Lisle* to draw up an ordinance for 500*l. per ann.* to be settled upon you and your heirs. This was done with smoothness; your friends were not wanting to you. I know thy burden; this is an addition to it: the Lord direct and sustain thee. Intelligence came to the hands of a very considerable person, that the

the King attempted to get out of his window, and that he had a cord of silk with him, whereby to flip down; but his breast was so big, the bar would not give him passage. This was done in one of the dark nights, about a fortnight ago. A gentleman with you led him the way, and flipped down. The guard, that night, had some quantity of wine with them. The same party assures, that there is *Aqua Fortis* gone down from *London* to remove that obstacle, which hindered; and that the same design is to be put in execution in the next dark nights. He saith, that captain *Titus* and some others about the King are not to be trusted. He is a very considerable person of the Parliament, who gave this intelligence, and desired it should be speeded to you.

The gentleman, that came out of the window, was Master *Firebrace* (*k*); the gentlemen

(*k*) *Henry Firebrace*, who was afterwards clerk of the kitchen to King *Charles* II. and whose *Narrative of certain Particulars relating to his Majesty* King Charles I. during

tlemen doubted are *Cresset, Burrowes,* and *Titus;* the time, when this attempt of escape was .... the twentieth of *March.*

Your Servant,

April 6th. 1648.   Oliver Cromwell.

For Col. R. Hammond, &c.

LETTER XV.

Mr. *Frost,* Secretary of the Committee of *Derby House,* to Col. *Hammond.*

SIR,

THERE is a new design to take away the King. *Firebrace, Titus,* and *Burrowes* are in it. *Burrowes* is either gone into *Sussex,* or about to go, to lie ready there at a place appointed. The other two are either gone, or on their way: they are to have a boat of four oars to bring

during the *Time,* that he attended on his *Majesty* at Newport *in the* Isle of Wight, *Anno* 1648. is published in p. 185. and seqq. of a volume printed at *London* 1702, in 8vo. under the title of *Memoirs of the two last Years of the Reign of that unparalleled Prince, of ever blessed Memory, King* Charles I.

off

off the King. The King hath a bodkin, with which he will raise the lead, in which the iron bar of the window stands, to put in the *Aqua Fortis* to eat out the iron. Then being got out, he will from the Bowlin Alley cast himself over the works, and so make his escape. Another design they have to fire the Castle, by firing a great heap of charcoal, that lies near the King's lodgings; and upon that tumult he to make his escape. I desire you to take special notice of it; for the King is extremely desirous to be abroad, hoping to be able to make such use of the present discontents, as to restore his affairs forthwith. The Committee not sitting, some of their members came in, and commanded, that thus much should be signified unto you from,

SIR,

Westminster, 15° *April*
 1658. Derby House, *Your most humble Servant,*
half an hour past one
in the afternoon.   Gualter Frost.

For his honoured friend Col. R. Hammond, *Governor of the* Isle *of* Wight.

LETTER

LETTER XVI.

To Col. *Hammond*. In Cypher.

SIR,

THERE is yet a design for the King's escape. Whensoever he shall attempt it, he will be assisted by * *Harrington*. Of the way we know nothing, nor have assurance, that this is true; but are only so informed. And this is written, that you may have the more watchful eye, and use your utmost care. You will be able to judge of the truth of this intelligence, if you do but examine, whether the King hath not lately had a relation or journal of all the proceedings of Sir *Thomas Bendish*, at *Constantinople*, and by whom he received it; as also, whether he hath not lately written letters to the *Muscovite*, in favour of the merchants trading thither; and by whom these letters were procured. If you find truth in either of these, you may

may believe, there is some also in the other.

18° *April* 1648.
For *Col.* R. Hammond, *Governor
of the* Isle of Wight.

LETTER XVII.

To Col. *Hammond.* In Cypher.

SIR,

BY a letter under the King's, hand he writes, that, although *Firebrace* and *Titus* be discovered, yet *D.* is fast to him, and will do the deed. This *D.* is one *Dowcett*, or such a name. There came 15 or 16 letters lately from the King, and those there of his party; 4 or 5 whereof were read by an honest man. The *Aqua Fortis* was spilt by the way by accident; but yesterday, about 4 o'clock, a fat plain man carried to the King a hacker, which is an instrument made here, on purpose to make the King's two knives, which he hath by him, cut as saws. The time assigned is *May Day* at night for the King's escape; but it may be sooner, if opportunity

tunity ferves. He intends to go firſt to a gentleman's houſe at *Lewes*, in *Suſſex*, who is thought to be a Parliament man. The man, that brings this hacker and difpatches, will go to *Newport*; and on *Saturday* morning, or about that time, *Dowcett*, *Harrington*, or ſome confidee, will go out and meet the man, and bring in all to the King. Therefore, if ſome occaſion be taken to ſearch them, as they return, all will appear.

Weſtminſter, 21°
April, 1648.   For your ſelf.

LETTER XVIII.

To Col. *Hammond*. In Cypher.

SIR,

YESTERDAY you had advice, that there was a fat plain man employed to carry the King an hacker; that he would go to *Newport* on *Saturday* morning; that there *Dowcett*, or *Harrington*, or ſome other, would meet him, and bring all to the King.

WE

WE have now from the same hand, that the same fat plain man comes no farther than *Portsmouth*, and from thence sends over his business by some fisherman, or some other such person, which will be received from him by some of the persons above-mentioned.

THE King is to write back divers letters, which will be brought to this man at *Portsmouth*, to be brought hither, and thence sent into *Scotland*. If therefore you cannot intercept those letters in the *Isle of Wight*, if you can send a faithful man, confident and discreet, to *Portsmouth*, who may be there on *Sunday* night, and diligently observe and enquire for such a man, who hath also a horse under him worth 30 *l.* or 40 *l.* (the colour we know not) and continue there till *Thursday*, he will certainly find such a man coming out of town with all the King's letters, whom he is to apprehend; and you are to send up the said letters hither with all security.

WE

We are farther informed, that there is a porter, who useth to carry up coals for the King's chamber presently after dinner and supper, who is to carry the King a disguise, which the King is to put on, and also the porter's frock, and to lock the porter into his chamber, and come down himself, whilst the servants are at supper; and so to pass away.

April 22d, 1648.

LETTER XIX.

To Col. *Hammond*. In CYPHER.

SIR,

THERE is an intention to get the King away to morrow at night, or *Thursday* morning; for *Sunday* a ship is fallen down from hence to *Queenborough*, where-abouts she rides, to waft him into *Holland*. Mrs. *Whorwood* (*l*) is aboard the ship,

(*l*) This lady is often mentioned with great expressions of confidence and respect by the King himself, in a collection of his letters, published in the Appendix to

ship, a tall, well-fashioned and well-languaged gentlewoman, with a round visage, and

to the 3d editition of Mr. *Thomas Wagstaffe's Vindication of King* Charles I. *the Martyr, proving that his Majesty was the author of* Εἰκὼν Βασιλικὴ, printed at *London* 1711. in 4to. The number of these letters is above sixty, the first being dated 12 *July*, and the last 30 *December* 1648. They were written to Sir *William Hopkins*, of *Newport*, in the *Isle of Wight*, Knt. and his son *George*, who were the first persons, that had declared and engaged for the King in that country, and whose house at *Newport* had been chosen by his Majesty for his residence during the treaty of the *Isle of Wight*. In these letters by the figure 39, as Mr. *Wagstaffe* remarks, p. 122. is evidently meant the King; by 48 the person, to whom he wrote; by 50, Col. *Hammond*; by *N*. most probably Mrs. *Whorwood*, who appears to have held a private correspondence by letters with his Majesty. She had likewise, if we believe *William Lilly*, the Astrologer, *History of Life and Times*, p. 60, 61, 62. come with the King's consent, while his Majesty was confined at *Hampton Court*, and had formed a resolution of escaping, to consult that Astrologer, in what quarter of the nation his Majesty might be safe, and not be discoverd till himself should think proper. *Lilly*, after the erection of a figure, told her, that about twenty miles from *London*, and in *Essex*, he was certain his Majesty might continue undiscovered. Mrs. *Whorwood*, upon this recollected a proper place in *Essex*, about that distance; but before she could reach *Hampton Court*, the King had left it, and was gone to the *Isle of Wight*. While his Majesty was prisoner in *Carisbrooke Castle*, and the *Kentish*

and pockholes in her face. She stays to wait upon the King.

A MERCHANT is gone from this town last night, or this morning early, to acquaint the King, that all things are ready: four horses lie in or near *Portsmouth* to carry the King by or near *Arundell*, and from thence to *Queenborough*. A Parliament-man, or one that was one, who liveth near *Arundell*, is to be the King's guide. The man is supposed be Sir *Edward Alford*. The merchant, that is come down to the King to *Portsmouth*, is a lean, spare young man. The place, by which the King is to escape, is a low room through a window, or a window, that is but slightly made up. He hath one or two about him, that are false. Have a special care of the King's bowling, lest he be suffered to escape under colour of bowling; which is the next plot. If this be

men took up arms for him, and several of the best ships revolted from the Parliament, a design being formed for his escape through his chamber-window, Mrs. *Whorwood* went again to *Lilly* for his advice, who procured G. *Farmer*, a Locksmith, in *Bow-Lane*, to make a saw to cut the iron-bars of the King's chamber asunder, besides furnishing a supply of *Aqua Fortis*.
prevented,

prevented, they will then have a ladder set up to the wall against the bowling-alley, and horses and a boat ready; and try that way.

The party, that gives this intelligence, saw lately a letter of the King's own hand, wherein he extreamly bemoans his condition, and resolves to attempt all means to free himself from it. The messenger, who last came, was so hard put to it by our intelligence, and your vigilance, that he was forced to leave his sword and pistols behind him, and durst not bring his letters to town; but one Doctor *Frazier* met him about *Windsor*, and took the letters of him.

4° *May* 48.

LETTER XX.

Col. *Hammond*, to the Committee of Lords and Commons.

My Lords and Gentlemen,

THE last night there came hither one *Job Weals*, a physician, as he calls himself, living at *Kingston upon Thames*.

He came hither upon poſt horſes, pretending to come in great haſt from my Lord General, imployed by him to me, on buſineſs of higheſt concernment. He counterfeited himſelf at firſt in a fainting fit, by reaſon of hard riding to me, and that he could not declare his buſineſs to me, until he had drank ſome hot water, to recover his ſpirits: which preamble being ill managed to his buſineſs, made me ſuſpect him to be a knave, as I afterwards more plainly found him. So ſoon as he feigned to come to himſelf, he began to tell me, that his buſineſs imported the ſafety of my life, and that, which was dearer to me, the great charge in my hands, the ſecurity of the perſon of the King; and to that end, I ſhould immediately remove the King to *Portſmouth* to Major *Lobb,* to whom he had directions to receive him: That otherwiſe the King would be violently taken hence the next morning, by 4 o'clock, and myſelf a dead man. For to his knowledge the deſign was ſo laid; and it was thus, that there was a fleet of ſhips at ſea near this coaſt, that were to come in between

tween the ifland and the lee fhore that evening, who were to land in the night, and that great numbers were to come out of the main land, pretending occafion at a fair, which was to be kept at *Newport* on the morrow, who fhould affift them; and at the fame time all the beacons in the ifland were to be fet on fire, and to raife the country for the King; and, if not, to amaze them with fear, that fo they might the better carry on their defign, which there was no way to avoid, but as he had given me direction. When he had concluded his tale, I enquired of him, whether he had any thing in writing to confirm it. He told me, that his inftructions to me were intrufted to him, to communicate only by word of mouth; but he had inftructions in writing quilted up in his waiftcoat for Major *Lobb*. I defired him to let me fee them: he told me, his order was only to communicate them to Major *Lobb*. I told him I muft fee them. He refufing, I told him, I apprehended he had other bufinefs here; and, if he would not immediately let me know it, I muft take another courſe with him. Whereupon I cauſed him to be ſtrictly ſearched, and found only theſe papers about him. That letter from him, without ſuperſcription or direction, he ſaith, was to my Lord of *Dover*; the reſt petitions and ſome notes of inſtructions of his own. When he found his idle plot would not take, and that he was diſcovered, he told me, he would deal ingenuouſly with me, and would tell me truly, his buſineſs was principally, by this means, to gain an intereſt with me, that ſo he might ſpeak with the King, to procure leave from him, that the county of *Surrey* (from whom he was ſent for that purpoſe) might have his Majeſty's approbation to chooſe a commander in chief, under whom to put their county in a poſture of defence. Upon his way he ſtoped a poſt going from *Portſmouth* to *London* with this incloſed packet; which, if your Lordſhips pleaſe, may be ſpeedily delivered, being about victual for the Navy. My Lords, I take this occaſion to let your Lordſhips know, that I wrote formerly to the General for a company or two of foot more, for the ſecurity

curity of this island from any sudden accident, that may happen from sea; which, it seems, he hath not thought fit to spare. I desire your Lordships, that, if you shall approve of it, there may be another company or two more raised, and maintained during this occasion some other way; and that some force, in the room of those lately removed thence, may be in *Hampshire*, near the water side, to be ready upon occasion to be transported hither. The two companies to be paid out of the remainder of the 30*l. per Diem*, I am now a raising; but fear I shall be much troubled myself with them, and the island more, by reason the mony comes not so constantly and truly, as were to be wished; for there is no keeping soldiers in very good order without money beforehand, where there is no free quarter. I desire also, for the better order of those companies here already, and to be raised, and for my own ease, if you shall think fit, I may have a Major under me, and pay allowed for him during this occasion.

sion. I desire it may be Capt. *Rolph* (*m*), who hath a company here already, who is
an

(*m*) Lord *Clarendon, History of the Rebellion,* b. xi. p. 560. remarks, that " this *Rolph* was Captain of a " foot company, whom *Cromwell* placed in the gar- " rison at *Carisbrooke Castle,* as a prime confident; " a fellow of a low extraction and very ordinary " parts, who, from a common soldier, had been " trusted in all the intrigues of the Army, and was " one of the agitators inspired by *Cromwell,* to put any " thing into the soldiers minds, upon whom he had " a wonderful influence, and could not contain him- " self from speaking maliciously and wickedly against " the King, when dissimulation was at the highest " amongst the officers." This *Rolph* was charged, in the beginning of *June* 1648. by Mr. *Richard Osborne,* Gentleman-Usher to the King, in a letter to *Philip* Lord *Wharton,* with a design of poisoning the the King; and that *Rolph* was favoured in it by Col. *Hammond* himself. [*Clarendon,* p. 560. and Sir *Philip Warwick's Memoirs,* p. 331, 332.] In answer to this charge, the Colonel sent a letter by Capt. *Rolph* to the House of Commons, in which he referred himself wholly to the King's knowledge, and to what his Majesty should say on that subject; and *Rolph* himself being called in, denied the said charge, and that he had ever discoursed with *Osborne* to the purpose alledg'd against him. The House upon this resolved the same day, the 23d of *June* 1648, that the Colonel's letter, with their order for giving freedom and security to *Osborne* for forty days, to make good the charge, should be printed. [*Rushworth,* part IV. vol. II. p. 1162.] On the 27th of that month *Osborne* appeared at the bar of the House of Lords, and

an honest, faithful, and careful man, and who taketh a great deal of pains, and deserves encouragement. The addition of Major's charged the matters contained in his letters against *Rolph* upon oath; and an impeachment was ordered to be drawn up thereupon. [Ibid. p. 1167.] On the 3oth the Lords sent a message to the Commons, that Mr. *Dowcett*, who had been committed to prison for endeavouring the King's escape out of the *Isle of Wight*, [Ibid. p. 1160.] might have liberty to attend their Lordships, as often as his testimony should be required in the business of *Rolph*; who was ordered by them to be committed prisoner to the *Gatehouse*, [ibid. p. 1171]. Col. *Hammond* wrote again to the House of Commons on the 4th of *July*, to urge, that the charge against *Rolph*, now a Major, might be brought to a speedy examination, " who, *says he*, I am confident, will
" appear a man exceedingly injured, and this only
" a design to work great disturbances in these di-
" stracted times. As this horrid scandal relates
" to the army, I must say, that neither directly nor
" indirectly from any member of it, or from any
" other person or persons whatsoever, did I ever re-
" ceive a word or tittle tending in the least to such
" a wicked purpose; much less as it relates to myself,
" could I, or did I, speak any such thing to Major
" *Rolph*. Herein I am satisfied, that in faithfulness
" and integrity I have served your commands, with
" all possible care of, and respect, to the person of
" the King. . . . And in this, I appeal to his Majesty,
" who of any man best knows it, and who doth,
" and, I doubt not, will still do, upon every occa-
" sion, as opportunity serves, sufficiently clear me."
[*Perfect Diurnal*, Nº. 259. *from* Monday 10 July *till*

Major's pay to his will be little, and not worth speaking off, but so much deserved by

Monday 17 July, 1648. p. 2082.] And on the 15th that month, a letter from *Carisbrooke Castle* written the day before was read in the House of Commons, that
" his Majesty had lately given before divers gentle-
" men of the Royal Party, a very honorable testi-
" mony of the governor, that he had been very civil
" and respectful in his carriage to him; that he was
" a man of honour and trust, and therefore they should
" not credit those scandalous stories, that were raised of
" him. This testimony his Majesty commanded them
" to declare to their friends; and the King having in-
" telligence of *Osborne's* having aspersed the gover-
" nor, was pleased to tell the latter, that as touching
" the preservation of his person from poison, or any
" other design, he was so confident of the honesty
" and faithfulness of the governor, that he thought
" himself as safe in his hands, as if he were in cus-
" tody of his own son." [Ibid.] But Sir *Philip Warwick* in his *Memoirs*, p. 330. is less favourable in his account of the King's sentiments of the governor some months after, about the time of the treaty of *Newport*. " I told the King, says Sir *Philip*, I un-
" derstood the governor usually prided himself in
" saying, that the person of the King was put into
" his hands by the Parliament; and that he would
" obey no directions concerning the same, but from
" the Parliament. *Now, Sir,* said I, *he is like to desire*
" *your leave to go up to them; but if you do, you know*
" *how Major* Rolph, *and other ill spirits of the Army,*
" *hang about this place; and what danger it may bring*
" *you: your Majesty, therefore, were best consider.* The
" King

by him, and such an officer so necessary for me, that makes me beg of your Lordships it may be moved in the house, if it

" King replied, *I thank you for your care; but the go-*
" *vernor is grown such a rogue, we cannot be in worse*
" *hands.* So I prest it no more; for (though not
" from himself) yet I had privately understood, he
" had at that time an hope to have escaped away by
" sea. But contrary winds, and contrary fortune,
" or rather Providence, made way for that, which tra-
" gically followed." And the King, himself in one of his letters to Sir *Willam Hopkins*, dated *Mond. after supper*, 21 *Aug.* 1648, has this passage: " You and
" *N.* [Mrs. *Whorwood*] have fully answered mine of
" yesternight; but a pox on 50 [Governor *Ham-*
" *mond*] for I think the devil cannot outgo him
" neither in malice, nor cunning. But, I believe be-
" fore this comes to you, you will hear more of his
" praise from *N.* to whom when you deliver this in-
" closed, desire her to return an answer as soon as she
" may." And in another letter dated *Wednesday morning August* 23d, his Majesty writes thus: " I
" have received *N.* [Mrs. *Whorwood's*] sad story; and
" seriously I could not have believed, that so much
" barbarity could have been in any body, that pre-
" tended to be a gentleman; and therefore in charity,
" I thought myself obliged to return her a consola-
" tory letter herewith." And in another of the same *Wednesday* night, " I thank you for the quick dispatch
" of my packet, and like very well your caution; for
" certainly all sort of barbarity is to be expected from
" 50 [*Hammond*] and it is some little consolation, that
" thus, in despite of him, I converse with those friends,
" with whom he debars me to speak."

cannot

cannot otherwife be done. Here is now but one fhip riding before this ifland for the guard of it, and the Captain of her hath this day fent me word, he is to go into victual upon *Wednefday* next. I defire, that care might be taken, that we may not in thefe times of trouble be without a fea-guard,

My Lords, from

Your Lordfhips moft faithful

And humble Servant,

Carifbrooke Caftle,
  May 22° 1648.   Ro. Hammond.

I PERCEIVE by difcourfes with him, that he hath been a great promoter of the late *Surrey* petition, and an agent of the malignants there.

LETTER XXI.

Mr. *Frost*, Secretary of the Committee of *Derby House*, to Col. Hammond, in CYPHER.

SIR,

THE design, of which I last wrote, still goes on. The ship lies in the *Isle of Sheppy*. I have again written to Col. *Rainsborough* of it. The time is to be *Thursday*, *Friday*, or *Saturday* night next, if opportunity serve them right, or about the 4th of *June*: the ways as formerly resolved on, of which you have formerly had notice. You desire subscriptions in these letters, which is not conceived necessary, being but of meer information.

I am, SIR,

Your most humble Servant,

Derby House, May 23, 1648.

Gualter Frost.

For his Honoured Friend Col. *Rob. Hammond*, Governor of the *Isle of Wight*, these are.

LETTER XXII.

The Committee at Derby House, to Col. Hammond.

SIR,

WE have received your two letters of the 29th and 30th of *May*, wherein we see the continuance of your great diligence and care in the discharge of your trust; of which as we are ourselves very sensible, so we shall be ready upon all occasions to represent it to your advantage.

We have appointed a report to the house, according to the desire of your letter, for 2 or 3000 *l.* to be sent unto you; and what shall be resolved therein, we shall use our best endeavour to expedite in the execution and dispatch. We have also written to the Lord General, and given him an extract of so much of your letters, as relates to the danger of the place, or need of forces, and defired his Lordfhip to give order for fupply therein.

The defection in the fleet (*n*) is only of two third rate fhips, and four frigates. They are in a mutinous temper among themfelves, and not like to agree together any long time. The Earl of *Warwick*, now Lord Admiral, hath been in the *Downs*; to whom they had in probability rendered themfelves, but that fome of the *Kentifh* men were aboard, and heightened the diftemper. His Lordfhip intends to come down to *Portfmouth*, and with what fhipping is there, and fuch as he can call to him of the Weftern fqua-

---

(*n*) Under the command of Real-Admiral *Rainfborough*, whom they had fet on fhore, and had fent to the Earl of *Warwick*, to take the command of them, and declared for King, Parliament, and Covenant. The Houfe of Commons referred this affair to the Committee of *Derby Houfe*; and, in compliance with the humours of the Revolters, voted, that the Earl of *Warwick* fhould be Lord High Admiral of *England*, and forthwith go to take care of the fleet. *Whitelocke*, p. 308.

dron,

dron, to take care of the security of the isle.

    Signed in the name, and by the warrant, of the Committee of Lords and Commons, at
Derby House, 1. *Derby House, by your affec-*
June, 1648. *tionate friend,*

         E. Manchester.
For Col. *Hammond.*

LETTER XXIII.

Instructions from Col. *Hammond,* to Major *Rolph.* &c.

BY reason of any accident, that may befal me in detaining me from the exercise of my duty, according to the trust reposed in me by the Parliament; my occasions and duty also calling me abroad into the island, I have thought fit to appoint, and hereby do appoint, Capt. *Boreman* and Major *Rolph* jointly, or, in the absence of any one of them, the other singly, to act all things in relation to the security of his Majesty's person, and this Castle, according to the instructions given

to

to that purpose, in as full and ample manner, as if myself were present: and, in case of such my absence, I also appoint Mr. *Herbert*, Mr. *Mildmay*, Mr. *Leigh*, treasurer, or any two of them, to take like care, and provide for the family in such way, as formerly by myself. And the said Capt. *Boreman* and Major *Rolph* for the soldiers, and Mr. *Herbert*, Mr. *Mildmay*, and Mr. *Leigh* for the family, are hereby farther desired by me so to act, until the Parliament shall please otherwise to determine the matter. In witness hereunto, I do hereto put my hand at *Carisbrook Castle*, this 2d of *June*, 1648.

Ro. Hammond.

Instructions for Major *Rolph*, Capt. *Boreman*, Mr. *Herbert*, Mr. *Mildmay*, and Mr. *Leigh*, in case I should be detained by any accident from doing my duty according to my instructions.

LETTER

LETTER XXIV.

The Committee at Derby House, to Col. Hammond.

SIR,

WE have received your letter; and before we had written to the General, and sent him a copy of your former letters, and represented to him our sense of the danger of the place, and desired him, that either from those forces with him, or from such other place as they might best be spared, some forces might be sent unto you. Upon the receipt of your last letter, we signified, in a postscript, that you had earnestly pressed for those supplies. For the money, that was ordered by the House, we suppose it is in a good forwardness; and that your agent will give an account of it in a day or two.

For the state of affairs, it stands thus: *Kent* is wholly reduced, except only the three castles in the *Downs*. One regiment of horse and one of foot is left there: the rest are all gone into *Essex* against the enemy there; with whom the Lord General also now is. Col. *Whalley* quartered last night, viz. the 11th at night, at *Witham*, which is 7 miles beyond *Chemlsford* toward *Colchester*. The enemy is not said to be 3000. The country, where they are not under the power of the enemy, are very cordial to the Army. For the fleet, of which you seem to be so much unsatisfied, we are informed the state stands thus: There are three ships at *Harwich*, two in the river of *Thames*, three ready to go out at *Chatham*, four, as you know, at *Portsmouth*, and three presently expected from the West. We are informed all these will be cordial, and we hope speedily got together; so as the danger is not like to be so great from the revolted fleet, as you seem to fear. Yet we shall not omit any thing in our power to provide for the security of that place of so great concernment.

> Signed in the name, and by the warrant, of the Committee of Lords and Commons, at Derby House, by your affectionate friend,

Derby House,
12 June. 1648.

Salisbury.

For Col. *Robt. Hammond*, Governor of the *Isle of Wight*.

LETTER XXV.

The Committee at *Derby House*, to Col. *Hammond*.

SIR,

FOR the greater security of the *Isle of Wight*, the House of Commons hath appointed, that five hundred of the Army shall be sent thither; and that the General shall recruit to the like number. We have sent the order to the Lord General, with a desire from this Committee, that the forces may be speedily sent thither; of which we thought fit to give you this advertisement, and have sent you also

alſo the copy of the order of the houſe incloſed.

Derby Houſe, 23 *Junii* 1647.

Signed in the name, and by the warrant, of the Committee of Lords and Commons at Derby Houſe, by your very loving friend,

Ed. Howard.

For Col. R. *Hammond,* Governor of the *Iſle of Wight.*

LETTER XXVI.

Col. *Hammond,* to the Committee of Lords and Commons.

My Lords and Gentlemen,

THOUGH I have often troubled your Lordſhips on this ſubject of farther ſupplies for the ſafety of the King's perſon, and this ſo conſiderable a place; yet my duty to yours, and the Kingdom's ſervice, put me upon it again, being thus occaſioned by an intelligence I have received, that the deſign of the revolted ſhips is (as it is very probable) to bring over men to invade this iſland; which if it ſhould ſo prove, the iſlanders, not being able to defend themselves, it is to be feared, may be forced to join with them: by which means they may become masters of the island; and so, having any considerable strength, may be able to keep off any forces of the Parliament, that may be sent for the relief of the Castle. My Lords, I therefore offer it to your Lordships' more serious consideration to take care of this place, so to possess it with a force of your own, as it may be able to keep off any other from landing, or getting footing in it; and, if to your Lordships' wisdoms it may seem fit, to possess the houses of Parliament with the concernment of it, so that a considerable force, both of horse and foot, may be sent over speedily for the defence of this island, and the preservation of the well-affected inhabitants of it, from the fury of their enemies, who are now so sensible of their danger, that they are both willing and desirous to receive farther force for the good of the kingdom and their own security, so that such provision may be certainly made for such force, as they may not be burthensome upon the country,

which

which, if it should be, would most certainly ruin them and the soldiers too. Which causeth me to make it my most humble and hearty suit to you, that, if the Parliament shall think fit to continue the person of the King in this island, and to send a sufficient force to provide for his security here, they may bring with them a considerable sum of money, for their present supplies: and that the assessments of the adjacent counties may be allowed for their future subsistance. This I humbly submit to your Lordships' consideration. My Lords, I understand, by some letters from private friends, that the two companies of the Army, concerning which I did formerly write to your Lordships, are by them thought to be already arrived in this island, or near it: but, as yet I have not heard from them, I humbly desire, that provision may be made for their subsistance and pay: otherwise it were better for me to be without them. I am, my Lords, your Lordships most humble and faithful servant,

Carisbrooke Castle,
June 23^d, 1648.   Ro. Hammond.

LETTER XXVII.

Col. *Hammond*, to the General *Thomas* Lord *Fairfax*.

My Lord,

YOUR excellency's great employments have been lately such, that I have not troubled you with the affairs of this place: but the concernment of them at this time is so considerable to the kingdom, that causeth me, amongst other your great affairs, to acquaint you with the danger this island is in, by reason of the late distemper of the Navy, by the revolt of it, whose design, as I am informed, and is very likely, is to bring over soldiers to invade this island; which if they should do, I being not able to prevent, or interrupt their landing, the islanders will be forced to join with them for their own preservation, which would impede the landing of any force for the relief of this Castle for the future. My desire therefore is, that, if the Parliament see fit to continue the person of the King in this place,

place, a very confiderable ftrength of horfe and foot, 300 horfe, and 1500 foot at the leaft, may be fpeedily fent over hither, to keep an enemy from landing. Horfe would be of excellent ufe here, becaufe no horfe can be brought to oppofe them. I have written to the Committee of *Derby Houfe* about this; and alfo, that, if they think it fit to fend fuch a force, that they be fure to provide a certain way for their pay; otherwife the country will immediately be eaten up. I hear nothing from the officers of the fecond company, I formerly wrote for, though from *London* I have been informed, that they have been long on their march hither. I hope they are the companies I formerly named to your Excellency, Capt. *Humphrey's*, and Capt. *Wheeler's*. It is of fpecial concernment to have fure men in the employment, they muft be ufed in; for, if they be otherwife, it will be too much in their power to undo me, and the kingdom alfo; as I was in danger to have found by late experience. My Lord, I thought it my duty to let your Excellency know our condition at prefent, present, it being of that general concernment; and do desire all furtherance from you, which I cannot but expect, as besides the public concernment of it, I have upon all occasions ever had so great testimony of your favour. My Lord, that the direction and presence of God may carry you through all your great affairs, is the hearty prayer of, my Lord,

Your Excellency's,

most faithful humble Servant,

Carisbrooke Castle,
23d *June*, 1648.

Ro. Hammond.

LETTER XXVIII.

Mr. *Frost*, Secretary of the Committee of *Derby House*, to Col. *Hammond*. In CYPHER.

SIR,

WE have credible information, that the Lord *Willoughby*, of *Parham* (*o*), hath a commission for Vice-Admiral of

(*o*) He had been, according to *Whitelocke*, p. 324. in the beginning of the troubles, very hearty and strong

the

the revolted ſhips, and is on board them. It is ſaid they have taken in 1000 ha- -men. They are to come to *Calais*, and thence to the *Iſle of Wight*. It was put in conſultation, whether they ſhould go to *Yarmouth*,

for the Parliament, and had manifeſted great perſonal courage, honour, and military as well as civil abilities; and was ſo high in the favour and eſteem of the Parliament, that they voted him to be General of the Horſe under the Earl of *Eſſex*, and afterwards to be an Earl. But he having taken a diſguſt at the Parliament's declining of a perſonal treaty with the King, and being jealous, that monarchy, and conſequently degrees and titles of honour, were in danger to be wholly aboliſhed, had been too forward in countenancing and aſſiſting the late tumults in the city, when the members of Parliament were drawn away from *Weſtminſter* to the Army. Upon the return of the members, he was, with other Lords, impeached of High Treaſon for that action; and rather than appear and ſtand a trial for it, he left his country, and revolted to the King, and joined the Prince in the Navy, for which the Houſe of Commons voted his eſtate to be ſecured. In 1650 his Lordſhip went to *Barbadoes*, where he aſſumed the title of Governor, and proclaimed King *Charles* II. (*Whitelocke*, p. 463, and 473); but in the year following he was obliged, by Sir *George Aſcue*, to ſurrender that, and the adjacent iſlands, to the obedience of the Common Wealth of *England* (Ibid. p. 527 and 521). In the latter end of *June* 1655, he and Lord *Newport* were committed to the *Tower* of *London*, upon ſuſpicion of treaſon,

[ibid

mouth, or to *Wight*; and the latter was concluded. They hold intelligence with some in the isle: they doubt not to effect their design.

June the last, at Ten at Night.   *Your humble Servant,*

Gualter Frost.

For his ever honoured friend Col. R. Hammond, *Governor of the* Isle of Wight, *these are.*

LETTER XXIX.

Mr. *Frost*, to his worthy friend Col. *Hammond*, Governor of the *Isle of Wight*. In CYPHER.

SIR,

THE Lord *Rich (p)* is with the King. The pretence is to be touched for the King's Evil, his disease being another.

ibid. p. 627,] but in *January* 1657-8, on presenting a petition to the Protector for leave to go into the country, to dispatch some necessary business relating to his estate, and promising to return to prison, he had leave granted, ibid. p. 660. After the restoration, he was was made Governor of the *Caribbee* islands; but lost his life in an hurricane near *Martinico* in *July* 1666.

(*p*) *Robert* Lord *Rich*, eldest son of the Earl of *Warwick*, Lord High Admiral under the long Parlia-

His

His business is to treat with him about the Earl of *Holland,* who is now General of a new army of desperadoes beginning to grow in *Surrey,* and for his father, and the rest of the fleet. You may judge of the truth of this by the former, given you in this way. You will see it was not feasible to have this signed by the Committee: you will make the best use of it you can. God direct you, who, I hope, will give wisdom in it, and uphold you in your most difficult employment. I hope, a few days will put us beyond any more of these plagues. The Prince is at *Calais;* all the old counsellors with him, many officers shipped to go to him. *Rossiter* hath fought and beaten his forces; slain many, and pursued them two days into *Leicestershire,* where *Loyney* fell on them. There are not three left: to either I owe intelligence.

Your humble Servant,

July 6, 1648.

Gualter Frost.

ment, whom Lord *Rich* succeeded in his titles and estate in 1658. His only son *Robert* married *Frances,* youngest daughter of the Protector *Oliver Cromwell*; but died before his father, who likewise deceased, 29 *May* 1659.

LETTER

LETTER XXX.

The Committee at Derby House, to Col. Hammond.

SIR,

THERE hath been for a good while many horses prepared in and about this town, that have been secretly sent into the country in small companies. They are now come together about *Kingston*, and it is said they are 500, or thereabouts, and many still come to them: it is said they intend to come to the *Isle of Wight*. There are many persons of great quality engaged in the design, and are now with them in person, *viz.* the Duke of *Buckingham*, and the Lord *Francis* his brother, the Earl of *Holland*, the Lord *Mollyneux*, and divers others. We have thought fit to give you this notice of their intention, that you might put yourself into a posture to prevent their landing; which, in regard of the few places they can land at, is supposed not difficult. If they bend

that

that way, we shall order such force, as we have in these parts, to follow them as close as we can. We desire you to give order, that the boats may be stayed on that side, that they may not have means to transport their men.

Signed in the name, and by the warrant, of the Committee of Lords and Commons, at Derby House, by your very loving friend,

Derby House, 5°. July, 1647. at 8 *at night.*

A. Northumberland.

For Col. R. Hammond, *Governor of the* Isle of Wight.

LETTER XXXI.

Commissary General *Ireton*, to Col. *Hammond*.

Dear ROBIN,

MY rare writing, I hope, will be excusable by our continual engagements, and not ordinary opportunities of sending by safe hands. For supply of strength, I hope thou hast not more need than we;

we, for a work so difficult, as here we have, for so small a force; though, through the goodness of God, we have pretty well overcome the difficulties, and rendered the remainder more easy. As to the charge in thy hands, and the difficult points thou mayst be put upon about it, I presume thou canst not be ignorant of the continued threats and menaces, and some apparent violences or attempts thereof, not from petitioners alone, but the rabble multitude and cavalierish party about *London,* and the parts adjacent; which most of the members of Parliament (if not the whole) have gone under, especially since the guards they had chosen, by whom they were protected in perfect freedom for the time, have been necessarily drawn off: Which threats and violences have been such, as have necessitated or given just occasion to very many (if not the most part) of those faithful members of the Commons House, by whom under God the interest of Parliament and Kingdom has been hitherto carried or upheld, and by whose votes, with others, this present charge was committed

to

to thee, to withdraw from their attendance at the Parliament, and repair home for their own and their country's safety. This, I can assure thee, the Army is sensible of, and, I hope, those will be. And so leaving thee to the best guidance and protection in the discharge of thy trust, I remain,

Thy entire friend to serve the,

League before Colchester,
July 9th, 1648.   H. Ireton.

To Col. R. Hammond, *Governor of the* Isle of Wight.

LETTER XXXII.

The Committee at *Derby House* to Col. Hammond.

SIR,

BY the enclosed extract from the letter of Dr. *Dorislaus*, which is also confirmed by other Letters for all the particulars of it, you see the state of the revolted ships; of which we thought fit to give you notice, that you might put yourself into the better posture against them, conceiving

ceiving it probable, they may bend their course towards the *Isle of Wight*. The Lord Admiral is now at *Chatham*, and will be ready to go forth in a very few days.

THE *Scots* came into *England*, on *Saturday* the 8th inst. with 72 colours of foot, and 27 colours of horse, certified by an express from Col. *Lambert*, who is at *Penrith*, with his forces. The House of Commons have thereupon passed the vote enclosed (*q*), which is sent away to Col. *Lambert*.

Signed in the name, and by the warrant, of the Committee of Lords and Commons at Derby House, by your very loving friend,

15ᵇ *July*, 1647.

For Col. *Rob.* Hammond, Governor of the *Isle of Wight*.

H. Kent.
LETTER

(*q*) " That the forces, that are now come out of
" *Scotland* into *England*, in an hostile manner, being
" without the authority of the Parliament of *England*,
" are enemies to the kingdom of *England*; and that
" all

LETTER XXXIII.

The Committee at *Derby House*, to Col. Hammond.

SIR,

WE have received information, that the revolted ships, who came to *Yarmouth*, the Prince being on board them, on *Saturday* last, and again the same day set sail from thence, having intention to go to *Portsmouth*, or the *Isle of Wight*; we have thought fit to give you this notice, and have written also to the Committee of *Hampshire*, and to the Committee of the *Isle of Wight*, if any such there be, to give you what assistance they can, in case of their arrival in the island. If there be no such Committee in the isle, there is no farther use to be made of that letter. We

" all such persons, either of this kingdom, or the
" kingdom of *Ireland*, that do, or shall hereafter, ad-
" here thereto, voluntarily aid, assist, or join with
" them, are rebels and traitors to the kingdom of
" *England*, and shall be proceeded against, and their
" estates confiscated as traitors and rebels." *Perfect Diurnal*, N° 259, *from* Monday 10th July, *to* Monday 17th July, 1648.

have also information, that there are letters conveyed to and from the King by the woman, who emptieth the stool; which letters are sent to *Boswell* (r), who lies on this side, not far from the isle; and they are sent by him to *Titus* (s), who is about,

(r) Sir *Tho. Herbert*, in his *Threnodia Carolina*, or *Memoirs*, published in 1702. p. 13. calls him *Major Bosvile*, and observes, that while the King resided at *Holdenby* or *Holmby*, in *Northamptonshire*, this Major had, in the disguise of a labouring man, delivered to his Majesty, as he passed over a bridge in going to *Harrowden*, a house of Lord *Vaux*, in the same county, a packet from the Queen. *Whitelocke*, p. 243. mentions also this fact; and adds, that the delivery of the packet was perceived only by a Miller, who stood by, and cried out, *Nobles and Gentlemen, there is a man gave his Majesty letters*; and that *Boswell* offered gold to the Miller to be silent, who would not take it. *Boswell* being seized, was ordered by the House of Commons, to be sent up to *London*, and was committed to *Newgate*. *Whitelocke*, p. 243, 246.

(s) *Silas Titus*, born at *Bushy*, in *Hertfordshire*, in 1622, and educated at *Christ Church, Oxford*, where he was entered a Commoner, in 1637, and resided about three years. He was at first a captain in the service of the Parliament; but after the death of King *Charles* I. he attended *Charles* II. to *Scotland*, and was with his Majesty, at the battle of *Worcester*. In 1657 he published, under the name of *William Allen*, a pamphlet, intitled, *Killing no Murder*, against *Oliver Cromwell*. At the Restoration, he was one of the Grooms of the Bed-

about, or not far from this town, and by him they are desperfed abroad.

27° *July*, 1648.

> *Signed in the name, and by the warrant, of the Committee of the Lords and Commons at Derby Houfe, by your affectionate friend.*

P. Wharton.

LETTER XXXIV.

The Committee at Derby Houfe to Col. Hammond. IN CYPHER.

SIR,

WE have information from a good hand, that there is an intention for the King to make efcape; the time to

---

Bed-chamber to the King, and a Colonel, and Member of Parliament, in which he fhewed great zeal in favour of the Bill of Exclufion; though after the Duke of *York* fucceeded to the Crown, the Colonel procured himfelf to be introduced in the beginning of *November* 1687 to the King, by *William Penn*, the *Quaker*, and on the 6th of *July* the year following, was fworn of his Privy Council. He was a man of very confiderable parts and wit, and lived to the age of eighty-two, dying in *December* 1704.

be on *Thursday* night, or *Friday* night; that he intends to land on this side at *Gosport*; that only two are to be in his company, a little antient man with a shrivelled face, and a lusty young man of about 26 or 27 years of age. We thought fit to give you this notice hereof, that you might thereupon with the greater diligence pursue your instructions from the Houses. We desire you to make your use of this information, but conceal the particulars to yourself, lest, if it be declared, it may also declare, by what means the information comes to us.

Signed in the name, and by the warrant, of the Committee of the Lords and Commons at Derby House, by your very affectionate friend.

13 *Nov.* 1648.

E. Manchester.

For Col. *R. Hammond*, &c.

LETTER

LETTER XXXV.

Commissary General *Ireton*, Major *Harrison*, Col. *Disbrowe*, and Col. *Grosvenor*, to Col. *Hammond*.

Sweet *Robin*,

OUR relation is so nigh upon the best account, that nothing can concern you or us, but we believe they are of a mutual concernment. And therefore we hold ourselves much obliged to transmit you this inclosed, coming from a sure hand to us; not only as relating to yours, or our particular, but likewise as a matter of vast importance to the public.

It hath pleased God (and we are persuaded in much mercy) even miraculously to dispose the hearts of your friends in the Army, as one man (together with the concurrence of the godly from all parts) to interpose in this treaty (*t*), yet in such wise, both for matter and manner, as, we believe,

(*t*) Between the King and Commissioners of the Parliament.

will not only refresh the bowels of the Saints, and all other faithful people of this kingdom; but be of satisfaction to every honest member of Parliament, when tendered to them, and made public; which will be within a very few days. And considering of what consequence the escape of the King from you (in the interim) may prove, we haste this dispatch to you, together with our most earnest request, that, as you tender the interest of this nation, of God's people, or of any moral men, or as you tender the ending of *England's* troubles, or desire, that justice and righteousness may take place, you would see to the securing of that person from escape, whether by returning of him to the Castle, or such other way, as in thy wisdom and honesty shall seem meetest.

We are confident you will receive in a few days a duplicate of this desire, and an assurance from the General and Army, to stand by you in it. And in the mean time, for our parts (though it may not be very considerable to you) we do hereby ingage
to

to own you with our lives and fortunes therein; which we should not so forwardly express, but that we are impelled to the premises in duty and conscience to God and man.

The Lord, your's and our God, be your wisdom and courage in this and all things. However, we have have done our duty, and witnessed the affection of,

Dear *Hammond*,

Windsor, 17th 9ber, 1648.

Your most entire and faithful

brethren, friends and servants,

H. Ireton,
T. Harrison,
John Disbrowe,
E. Grosvenor.

For our honourable friend Col. Robert Hammond, *these*.

LETTER XXXVI.

The Committee at *Derby House*, to Col. *Hammond*.

SIR,

SINCE our last we have received again an advertisement from a good hand, that the design holds for the King's escape (*u*); and to escape all suspicion from you, he intends

(*u*) Though the King, when he wrote to the Parliament, that he was ready to treat with the Commissioners, which should be named by them, at *Newport*, in the *Isle of Wight*, engaged his Royal Word, as Sir *Thomas Herbert* remarks, *Memoirs*, p. 69. that *he would not depart out of the* Isle of Wight *during the Treaty, which was limited to six weeks time, nor in three weeks after*; yet it appears from the letters of his Majesty to Sir *William Hopkins*, cited above, note [*l*], that very soon after the treaty began he had thoughts of making his escape. In a letter, dated *Saturday* night, *October* 7. *Appendix*, p. 160. he says, " Though I " doubt not of your care in expediting that business, " whereof I spoke to you this morning; yet I can- " not but tell you, that you cannot make ready too " soon; for by what I have heard since I saw you, " I find, that few days will make that impossible, " which now is feasible. Wherefore, I pray you " give me an account as soon as you can; first where " I shall take boat? Spare not my walking in re-
" spect

intends to walk out on foot a mile or two, as ufually, in the day time, and there horfes are laid in the ifle to carry him to a boat.

"If fpect of fecurity. Then how the tide falls out? Or, whether in cafe the wind do ferve, it be neceffary to look to the tides? What winds are fair? What may ferve? And what are contrary? Confider alfo if a pafs from 50 [*Hammond*] may not be ufeful? Laftly, how foon all will be ready, and what the impediments are, which refts? I fhall order the time of night as you fhall judge moft convenient." The fame point is touched upon in the letters of *Sunday* at night, 8 *October*, and of *Monday* night, 9 *October*, p. 160, 161; in the latter of which the King writes thus: "I pray you rightly to underftand my condition; which, I confefs, yefternight I did not fully enough, through want of time. It is this: Notwithftanding my too great conceffions already made, I know, that unlefs I fhall make yet others, which will directly make me no King, I fhall be at beft but a perpetual prifoner. Befides, if this were not, of which I am too fure, the adhering to the church, from which I cannot depart, no not in fhew, will do the fame. And, to dealy freely with you, the great conceffion I made this day, [*relating to the Church, Militia, and Ireland*; See Sir *Edward Walker's Perfect copies of all the votes, letters, propofals, and anfwers in the treaty in the* Ifle of Wight, p. 49, 54.] was made merely in order to my efcape: of which if I had not hope, I would not have done; for then I could have returned to my ftrait prifon without reluctancy. But now, I confefs, it would break my heart, having done that,

"which

If he cannot do this, then either over the houfe in the night, or at fome private window

"which only an efcape can juftify. To be fhort, if I
"ftay for a demonftration of their farther wickednefs,
"it will be too late to feek a remedy: for my only
"hope is, that now they believe that I dare deny
"them nothing, and fo be lefs careful of their guards.
"Wherefore, as you love my fafety, let us difpatch
"their bufinefs as foon as we can, without expecting
"news from *London*: and let me tell you, that if I
"were once abroad and under fail, I would willing-
"ly enough hazard the three pinnaces. To con-
"clude, I pray you believe me (and not the common
"voice of mankind) that I am loft, if I do not efcape,
"which I fhall not be able to do, if, as I have faid,
"I ftay for farther demonftrations. Therefore, for
"God's fake, haften with all diligence you can, and
"give a daily account to 39" [*the King himfelf*). In the letter on *Tuefday afternoon October* 10, his Majefty fays, "What I wrote yefternight, was not to add
"fpurs, but really to give you the true ftate of my
"condition; and as I have freely trufted you with the
"greateft fecret I have, in regard to your fidelity,
"for the feafibility I fhall truft to your judgment.
"It were a wrong to my confidence and your dili-
"gence, more to exhort you. Wherefore this is
"only to tell you, that I find it neceffary to acquaint
"this bearer, *George Kirke*, my oldeft and moft trufty
"fervant, with this great fecret, both to eafe my
"pains of writing, and for the better adjufting of all
"particulars. And fo I refer you to what he fhall
"fay to you from 39." The King adds in a poft-fcript, *The procuring of a Dutch Pink would make all fure*.

window in the night, he intends his paſſage; which we thought fit again to give
you

ſure. Another letter, p. 162. dated *Thurſday night after ſupper*, 9 *November*, contains this paſſage:
" I ſhould be very ſorry, that your expoſing yourſelf
" to this Eaſtern wind ſhould do you any harm; but
" it will make me the more beholden to you, nor
" ſhall I forget your daily pains and hazards for my
" ſervice. In the mean time, I hope, that the wind,
" which probably may bring me good luck, will do
" you no harm. At this time I will ſay no more,
" but if the ſhip come, I like that way beſt; yet if ſhe
" come not quickly, I muſt take ſome other way;
" for I daily find more and more reaſon to haſten;
" and even ſince ſupper, I have it from a ſure intelli-
" gence, that the buſineſs of *Ireland* will break all.
" Wherefore, I muſt ſtay no longer than towards the
" end of next week, if ſo long. So that you muſt
" act accordingly; and upon *Levet's* return, which
" I hope will be on *Saturday*, I muſt ſet a day." And
in the next letter p. 163. dated *Sunday*, 12 *November
after ſupper*, the King tells the ſame correſpondent,
mark'd by the figures 48, " That you may give me the
" fuller account to-morrow at night, I deſire you to
" inform yourſelf of the tides, and alſo of the Horſe-
" guards, both how they are placed, and what rounds
" they ride. This is all now; but when you come,
" I will propoſe ſome conſiderations unto you how to
" prevent accidents." Among theſe letters, is inſert-
ed, p. 158, 159, one by another perſon, ſubſcribed
by a counterfeit name, and written either to the King
himſelf, or to the King's correſpondent; in which
what relates to a deſign againſt his Majeſty's perſon,

you notice of, that you may make such use of for prevention, as you shall see cause.

> Signed in the name, and by the warrant, of the Committee of Lords and Commons at Derby House, by your very affectionate friend,

Derby House,
18 *Nov.* 1648.

Salisbury.

is in Cypher; but decyphered by the King's own hand. The letter is among those of the King's, dated in *October* 1648. The most remarkable passage is as follows: " There is *a notable design, to which are agreed* " *the Army and Parliament*; and by concurring coun- " sels; to which end, *an Express is sent to* Cromwell, *to* " *dispose of his Majesty*. Many here wish (for his " friends in the city are numerous) that the King " would thoroughly concede, to prevent dangers in- " cumbing. But, I fear, if good be not intended " him, no condescension of his can abort it. *If then* " *he will betake him to his escape, let him do it on Thurs-* " *day or Friday next*, but by all means, *out of some* " *door, and not from the top of the house* by the help of lad- " ders. For I have heard too much of that way talked " of *by some near him*. Farther, I desire none may be " trusted herewith, but *your Son and Levet*. *The Prince* " *of Orange will not fail*, I know, to send *a ship*; but " I have too great reason to apprehend, if he rely " thereon, his intention will be made frustrate, as not " coming time enough. I have given some overtures " to him, which you, giving him the sense, or sight " of this letter, may, as you see cause, advance."

LETTER XXXVII.

Commissary General *Ireton*, to Col. *Hammond*.

Dear *Robin*,

THOU wilt receive herewith a letter from the General (*w*), by which thou wilt see what tenderness there is here towards thee. I shall not at this distance

(*w*) He, as appears from *Rushworth*, part II. vol. II. p. 1338, wrote a letter to Col. *Hammond*, requiring his attendance at the head-quarters, and acquainting him, that Col. *Ewer* was appointed to take the custody of his Majesty in the *Isle of Wight*. This letter being transmitted from Col. *Hammond* by Major *Cromwell* to the House of Commons, they resolved, on *Monday* the 27th of *November*, 1648, upon the receipt of it, that he should be required to stay in the *Isle of Wight*, and attend his charge there till farther order, and that the General should be acquainted with this vote. They resolved likewise to send a letter to the Lord Admiral, to require him to send some ships to that island, with orders for them to obey the command of Col. *Hammond*. The evening before, a messenger had brought word to *Windsor*, that Col. *Ewer* had the custody of his Majesty; and that Col. *Hammond* was upon his way to *Windsor* [*Whitelocke*, p. 357.] whence he sent letters, on the 30th of *November*, to the Parliament by Major *Cromwell*, that he was

distance undertake a dispute concerning our ground or proceedings; but leave thee for the one to our *Remonstrance*; for the other to farther tryal of us. I shall only, in the love of a friend and brother, speak a word or two to that, which I find the ground of thy scruples against what hath

was detained there [Ibid. p. 358]. The treaty with the King having been prolonged to the 27th of *November*, the Commissioners for the Parliament returned to *London* the day following; and on the 30th the soldiers sent from the Army under Lieut. Col. *Cobbet* seized the King at *Newport*, and the next morning carried him to *Hurst Castle*. The army marched to *London*, the 2d of *December* following; and upon House of Commons having on *Tuesday* the 5th voted, after a very long debate, that his Majesty's answers to the propositions of both Houses, in the treaty of the *Isle of Wight*, were a ground to proceed upon for settling the peace of the kingdom, a body of foot, under Col. *Pride* and other officers, on the 6th, put a force on the house, seizing and imprisoning forty three members, who had concurred in that vote, forcibly secluding above an hundred more that day and the next, and pulling two out of the house, who had got in before they were perceived by the officers. *A full declaration of the true state of the secluded members case*, p. 14. edit. *London*, 1660, 4to. The issue of this violence was the King's being brought, by order of the Army, to *Windsor*, and thence to *London*, which was soon followed by his tryal and execution.

been

been from hence defired, or rather of thy declared refolution to the contrary.

Thou lookeſt on thyſelf as a ſervant under truſt; and ſo both in honour and conſcience obliged to diſcharge that faithfully. And thus far thou art in the right. But the only meaſure of that diſcharge thou takeſt to be the mere formal obſervance of commands; and thoſe carrying but that name of power, from which thou apprehendeſt it was committed to thee. As to the firſt part, the faithful diſcharge of the truſt, the Lord forbid, that I ſhould tempt thee from it. Nay, I will charge and challenge it at thy hands, that, with all faithfulneſs and ſingleneſs of heart, as before the Lord, thou perform thy truſt to thoſe perſons, by whom, and to thoſe public ends and intereſts, for which, it was committed to thee.

But for theſe things, I ſhall appeal to the witneſs of God in thy conſcience, as follows:

G   I. For

I. For the persons trusting, whether thou didst receive thy present place from the affections or trust of the formal Parliament only, even as then it stood; or whether of the General or Army? And whether, so far as thou seemest to have the formality by way of confirmation from the Parliament, it were from any affection or trust of that sort or generation of men, which now, through accident, bear the sway and name? Or whether from them, whose judgment and affections are most opposite to the present proceedings there?

II. For the ends, whether thou receivedst thy trust in order to the ends now carried on by the prevailing party there? Or whether, in confidence of thy faithfulness, to some other higher and more public ends? Whether for the King's, and the present prevailing faction's; or for the public interest, and the generality of honest men, that have engaged for the same.

Upon the anfwer of thy confcience in thefe, I propound farther; in cafe fuch perfons, as neither did, nor would have committed any fuch truft unto thee, but only gaining fince the name of that power, from which thou hadft the formal compliment of the truft, and yet but partly that, fhall require things deftructive to, or not for the beft advantage of, thofe public ends, for which realy thou receivedft thy truft; and at the fame time thofe, from whofe affection and confidence in thee thou hadft the matter of thy power and truft, fhall defire and expect from thee other things neceffary for the fecurity, or but really for better advantage, of thofe public ends, for which thou wert trufted, and for the common benefit and intereft of that people, for which all pretend their employments and intereft; in this cafe, I fay, I fhall appeal farther to thy confcience, or but ingenuity, to determine, to which of thefe feveral perfons, and according to which commands and expectations, thou art to exhibit and approve thy faithfulnefs in the truft: And whether part to obferve and follow is the more real and fubftantial performance before God, and reafonable men.

I shall not prefs upon thee, but thus plainly lay the cafe before thee; only defiring thee not to flight it, but ferioufly weigh it, as thou tendereft the approving thyfelf to God and his people. And, I hope, he will not give thee up to fuch delufion, as to follow an air of honour, and mere form or fhadow of faithfulnefs, to the rejection or neglect of that, which is the reality and fubftance of both, as furely thou wouldft, if in the prefent cafe thou fhouldft neither do the thing expected thyfelf, nor leave it to any other.

Dear *Robin*, I will yet hope God hath better endued thee with truth and judgement in the inner parts, and more fenfe of his righteous judgments appearing abroad in this age and nation. So I leave thee to his gracious guidance; and the weight of what I have writ, lying not in authority to indemnify thee, but reafon to lead

lead thee. I shall not need to subscribe other name than, what I must desire to be known by unto thee,

Thy most dearly

Affectionate and faithful

Friend to serve thee.

Nov. 22d, 1648.

For my dear Friend Col. Hammond, *Governor of the* Isle of Wight.

LETTER XXXIX.

Oliver Cromwell, to Col. *Hammond.*

Nov. 25. 1648.

Dear *Robin*,

NO man rejoyceth more to see a line from thee, than myself. I know thou hast long been under tryal. Thou shalt be no loser by it. All must work for the best. Thou desirest to hear of my experiences. I can tell thee, I am such a one, as thou didst formerly know, having a body of sin and death; but, I thank God, through Jesus Christ our Lord, there is no condemnation, though much infirmity, and I wait for the redemption; and in this poor condition I obtain mercy and sweet consolation through the Spirit; and find abundant cause every day to exalt the Lord,—abase flesh. And herein I have some exercise.

As to outward dispensations, if we may so call them; we have not been without our share of beholding some remarkable providences and appearances of the Lord. His presence hath been amongst us, and by the light of his countenance we have prevailed. We are sure, the good will of him, who dwelt in the bush, has shined upon us; and we can humbly say, we know in whom we have believed, who is able, and will perfect what remaineth, and us also in doing what is well-pleasing in his eye-sight.

Because I find some trouble in your spirit, occasioned first, not only by the continuance of your sad and heavy burthen, as you call it, upon you; but by the

the dissatisfaction you take at the ways of some good men, whom you love with your heart, who through this principle, that it is lawful for a lesser part (if in the right) to force, &c.

To the first : Call not your burthen sad nor heavy. If your father laid it upon you; he intended neither. He is the father of lights, from whom comes every good and perfect gift; who of his own will begot us, and bad us count it all joy when such things befall us; they being for the exercise of faith and patience; *whereby in the end (James i.) we shall be made perfect.*

Dear *Robin,* our fleshly reasonings ensnare us. These make us say; *heavy, sad, pleasant, easy:* Was not there a little of this, when *Rob. Hammond,* through dissatisfaction too, desired retirement from the Army, and thought of quiet in the *Isle of Wight.* Did not God find him out there? I believe he will never forget this.—And now I perceive, he is to seek again, partly through his sad and heavy burthen,

and partly through diffatisfaction with friend's actings. Dear *Robin*, thou and I were never worthy to be door-keepers in this fervice. If thou wilt feek, feek to know the mind of God in all that chain of providence, whereby God brought thee thither, and that Perfon to thee: How before and fince God has ordered him, and affairs concerning him. And then tell me, whether there be not fome glorious and high meaning in all this, above what thou haft yet attained. And laying afide thy fleshly reafon, feek of the Lord to teach thee what that is; and he will do it. I dare be pofitive to fay; it is not, that the wicked fhould be exalted, that God fhould fo appear, as indeed he hath done. For there is no peace to them: No, it is fet upon the hearts of fuch as fear the Lord, and we have witnefs upon witnefs, that it fhall go ill with them, and their partakers. I fay again, feek that fpirit to teach thee; which is the fpirit of knowledge and underftanding, the fpirit of counfel and might, of wifdom and of the fear of the Lord. That fpirit will
clofe

close thine eyes, and stop thine ears, so that thou shalt not judge by them; but thou shalt judge for the meek of the earth; and thou shalt be made able to do accordingly. The Lord direct thee to that, which is well pleasing in his eye sight.

As to thy dissatisfactions with friend's actings upon that supposed principle, I wonder not at that. If a man take not his own burthen well, he shall hardly others; especially if involved by so near a relation of love and christian brotherhood, as thou art. I shall not take upon me to satisfy; but I hold myself bound to lay my thoughts before so dear a friend. The Lord do his own will.

You say; " God hath appointed au-
" thorities among the nations, to which
" active or passive obedience is to be
" yielded. This resides in *England* in the
" Parliament. Therefore active or pas-
" sive, &c."

AUTHORITIES and powers are the ordinance of God. This or that species is of
human

human inftitution, and limited, fome with larger, others with ftricter bands, each one according to its conftitution. I do not therefore think, the authorities may do any thing, and yet fuch obedience due; but all agree, there are cafes, in which it is lawful to refift. If fo, your ground fails, and fo likewife the inference. Indeed, Dear *Robin*, not to multiply words, the query is, whether ours be fuch a cafe? This ingenuoufly is the true queftion. To this I fhall fay nothing, though I could fay very much; but only defire thee to fee what thou findeft in thy own heart as to two or three plain confiderations: *Firft*, Whether *Salus Populi* be a found pofition? *Secondly*, Whether in the way in hand, really and before the Lord, before whom confcience muft ftand, this be provided for; or the whole fruit of the war like to be fruftrated *(y)*, and all moft like

---

(y) This argument is fully dilated upon in p. 35. & feqq. of the *Remonftrance of his Excellency* Thomas Lord Fairfax, *Lord General of the Parliament forces, and of the general council of officers held at St.* Alban's, *the* 16*th of* November, 1648. *prefented to the Commons affembled*

like to turn to what it was, and worſe. And this contrary to engagements, declarations, implicit covenants with thoſe, who ventured their lives upon thoſe covenants and engagements, without whom perhaps, in equity, relaxation ought not to be.

Thirdly, Whether this Army be not a law-

aſſembled in Parliament the 20*th inſtant, and tendered to the conſideration of the whole kingdom :* Printed at *London,* 1648, in 4to. This *Remonſtrance* demanded, that the perſon of the King might be proceeded againſt in way of juſtice, and a peremptory day ſet for the Prince of *Wales* and Duke of *York* to come in and render themſeleves, and, if they did not, to be declared traitors: That a period be ſet to this Parliament, and a proviſion made for a new and more equal repreſentative of the people : And that no King might hereafter be admitted, but upon the election of, and as upon truſt for, the people, by ſuch their repreſentatives. The *Remonſtrance,* being preſented to the Houſe of Commons by Col. *Ewer* and other officers, occaſioned a long and high debate; ſome members inveighing ſharply againſt the inſolence of it; others palliating and excuſing the matters in it, which ſome did not ſcruple to juſtify; while moſt were ſilent, becauſe it came from the Army, and feared, that the like would be done by them, of what had been formerly. At laſt the debate was adjourned to the 30th of *November,* when the queſtion being put, whether the *Remonſtrance* ſhould be taken into ſpeedy conſideration, it was by ninety voices reſolved in the negative. *Whitelocke,* p. 355 and 357.

full

ful power, called by God to oppose and fight against the King upon some stated grounds; and being in power to such ends, may not oppose one name of authority for those ends as well as another? the outward authority, that called them, not by their power making the quarrel lawful; but it being so in itself. If so,—it may be, acting will be justified in *Foro humano*. But truly these kind of reasonings may be but fleshly, either with or against; only it is good to try what truth may be in them. And the Lord teach us.

My dear friend, let us look into providences; surely they mean somewhat. They hang so together — have been so constant, so clear and unclouded.—Malice, swol'n malice against God's people, now called Saints, to root out their name. And yet they by providence having arms; and therein blessed with defence, and more.

I desire, he, that is for a principle of suffering, would not too much slight this.

I

I flight not him, who is fo minded; but let us beware, left flefhly reafoning fee more fafety in making ufe of the principle, *than in acting.* *Who acts, and refolves not through God to be willing to part with all?* Our hearts are very deceitful on the right and on the left. What think you of providence difpofing the hearts of fo many of God's people this way, efpecially in this poor Army, wherein the great God has vouchfafed to appear. I know not one officer amongft us, but is on the increafing hand: And let me fay, it is *here in the North, after much patience,* we truft the fame Lord, who hath framed our minds in our actings, is with us in this alfo. And this, contrary to a natural tendency, and to thofe comforts, our hearts could wifh to enjoy with others. And the *difficulties* probably to be encountred with, and enemies, not few, even all, that is glorious in this world, with appearance of united names, titles, and authorities, and yet not terrified, only defiring to fear our great God, that we do nothing againft his will. Truly this is our condition.

AND

AND, to conclude, we in this Northern Army were in a waiting posture, desiring to see what the Lord would lead us to. And a declaration is put out, at which many are shaken; although we could perhaps have wished the stay of it, till after the treaty: yet, seeing it is come out, we trust to rejoyce in the will of the Lord, waiting his farther pleasure. Dear *Robin*, beware of men, look up to the Lord. Let him be free to speak, and command in thy heart. Take heed of the things, I fear thou hast reasoned thyself into; and thou shalt be able through him, without consulting flesh and blood, to do valiantly for him and for his people. Thou mentionest somewhat, as if by acting against such opposition, as is like to be, there will be a tempting of God. Dear *Robin*, tempting of God ordinarily is either by acting presumptuously in carnal confidence, or in unbelief through diffidence: both these ways *Israel* tempted God in the Wilderness, and he was grieved with them. The encountring difficulties therefore makes us us not to tempt God; but acting before, and without faith. If the Lord have in any meafure perfuaded his people, as generally he hath, of the lawfulnefs, nay of the *duty*; this perfuafion prevailing upon the heart is faith, and acting thereupon is acting in faith, and the more the difficulties are, the more faith. And it is moft fweet, that he, that is not perfuaded, have patience towards them that are, and judge not; and this will free thee from the trouble of others actings; which, thou fayeft, adds to thy grief. Only let me offer two or three things, and I have done.

Doest thou not think, that fear of the Levellers (of whom there is no fear) that they would deftroy nobility, had caufed fome to rake up corruption, to find it lawful to *make this ruining hypocritical agreement* (on one part). Hath not this biafled even fome good men? I will not fay, their fear will come upon them; but if it do, they will themfelves bring it upon themfelves. Have not fome of our friends by their paffive principle (which I judge not,

only

only I think it liable to temptation as well as the active; and neither good, but as we are led into them by God—neither to be reasoned into, because the heart is deceitful) been occasioned to overlook what is just and honest; and think the people of God may have as much, or more good the one way, than the other. Good by this man! against whom the Lord hath witnessed; and whom thou knowest. Is this so in their hearts, or is it reasoned, forced in?—*Robin*, I have done. Ask we our hearts, whether we think, that, after all these dispensations, the like to which many generations cannot afford, should end in so corrupt reasonings of good men; and should so hit the designings of bad? Thinkest thou in thy heart, that the glorious dispensations of God point out to this, or to teach his people to trust in him, and to wait for better things, when, it may be, better are sealed to many of their spirits? And as a poor looker on, I had rather live in the hope of that spirit, and take my share with them, expecting a good issue, than be led away with the other

other. This trouble I have been at, because my soul loves thee, and I would not have thee swerve, nor lose any glorious opportunity the Lord puts into thy hand. The Lord be thy counsellor. Dear *Robin*,

I rest thine,

O. Cromwell.

Nov. 25, 1648.

F I N I S.

www.ingramcontent.com/pod-product-compliance
Lightning Source LLC
Chambersburg PA
CBHW030401170426
43202CB00010B/1454